The Heart of
LONELINESS

How Jewish Wisdom Can Help You Cope and Find Comfort

RABBI MARC KATZ

Foreword by Rabbi Danya Ruttenberg

For People of All Faiths, All Backgrounds

JEWISH LIGHTS Publishing

Nashville, Tennessee

Skylight Paths Publishing
an imprint of Turner Publishing Company
Nashville, Tennessee
New York, New York

www.skylightpaths.com
www.turnerpublishing.com

The Heart of Loneliness:
How Jewish Wisdom Can Help You Cope and Find Comfort

For information regarding permission to reprint material from this book, please mail or fax
your request in writing to Jewish Lights Publishing, Permission Department, at the address / fax
number listed below, or e-mail your request to submissions@turnerpublishing.com.

Library of Congress Cataloging-in-Publication Data
Names: Katz, Marc, Rabbi, author.
Title: The heart of loneliness : how Jewish wisdom can help you cope and find comfort /
    Rabbi Marc Katz ; foreword by Danya Ruttenberg.
Description: Woodstock, VT : Jewish Lights Publishing, [2016] I Includes bibliographical
    references.
Identifiers: LCCN 2016025734I ISBN 9781580238717 (pbk.) I ISBN 9781580238816
    (ebook)
Subjects: LCSH: Loneliness. I Loneliness—Religious aspects—Judaism. I Faith (Judaism)
Classification: LCC BF575.L7 K38 2016 I DDC 296.7/6—dc23 LC record available at
    https://lccn.loc.gov/2016025734

10 9 8 7 6 5 4 3 2 1

Manufactured in the United States of America
Cover Design: Jenny Buono
Cover Art: © Eugenio Marongiu/shutterstock.com
Interior Design: Thor Goodrich

For Ayelet, my constant source of strength

Contents

Foreword

The irony of loneliness: it pervades all of our lives at times and yet is so often something of a taboo subject. When we encounter people in synagogue or at work, the answer to the question, "How are you?" is almost never, "Well, actually, I'm feeling pretty forlorn right now." We rarely post about feeling estranged on social media. A lot of the time, maybe, we don't even really admit our lonely feelings to ourselves. But they're there nonetheless.

There are so many ways in which we become isolated or alienated. Maybe we're navigating a time of challenge or life upheaval; maybe we've changed somehow and just don't feel the same sense of connection to the people to whom we once felt close; maybe it's something as simple as the fact that just being a human being in the world is really hard sometimes.

But we don't have to be alone in our loneliness. Rabbi Marc Katz has written a powerful, important book on the ways in which the Jewish tradition speaks to, understands, and offers a way out of isolation. It's a book about the solace that we can find connecting with the deep spiritual insights of our textual heritage and, most importantly, how we can move from desolation into true connection with others. It offers a pathway into relationship and authentic community, into being truly seen for who we are—and learning to respond to others with love and care as well.

This book is invaluable for anyone who feels lonely even some of the time—that is to say, for all of us. And it's absolutely necessary reading for the Jewish world as a whole. Synagogues and other communities may feel as though they're doing a good job at building strong collective ties but attendance at events is not a fair indicator of whether the people who show up feel, ultimately, as though they matter.

There are a lot of ways that we can create bonds of connection and love to cure the loneliness that is so painfully pervasive these days. This book is the way in—and through—that pain. Jerusalem was a city "once great with people," Lamentations tells us. So too can be our lives when we all learn how to find one another once again.

Introduction

As a child, I often heard the story of Honi the Circle Maker around Tu Bishvat (Talmud, *Taanit* 23a). One day Honi is walking down the street when he meets an old man who is planting a carob tree. Honi asks the man how long the tree will take to bear fruit. "Seventy years," says the man. Mocking him, Honi asks why he would plant a tree that he might never eat from. The old man replies, "I was born into a world with carob trees, and just as my ancestors planted trees for me, so too will I plant them for my children."

Immediately Honi eats a meal and falls asleep for decades. Upon awaking, Honi sees a man gathering fruit. "Did you plant that tree?" he asks, noticing a tree where there had not been one before. "No," says the man. "It was my grandfather." At that moment, Honi learns that he had slept for seventy years.

This story teaches us about environmental stewardship, humility, and respect for future generations. Yet, like many stories in our tradition, the story we tell our children falls short of conveying the whole tale. It wasn't until I was an adult that I learned how the story ended. Upon waking up, Honi begins wandering the town. He learns that in the seventy years that he has been asleep people have already mourned his death. His son, who was a child before his lengthy slumber, has also passed away. His oldest remaining relative is his grandson.

When he tries to tell the villagers that he is indeed Honi, no one will believe him. Feeling rejected, Honi goes to the place where he felt most at home before this ordeal, the communal study hall. Yet even there Honi cannot convince his rabbinic colleagues of his identity. Time and again, they make reference to his teachings. They cite his previous legal rulings and interpretations to prove points in their arguments. His presence is felt acutely in the hall, but he is invisible. They neither believe him when he reveals himself nor give him his due honor.

Honi has seen the future. His legacy is secured. For generations people have embraced Honi's intellect and thoughtfulness, invoking both in their instruction. Yet that is not enough. They cannot see him in his fullest identity. Invisible, he is alienated not only from them but also from himself. He cannot live in a world of such isolation. He prays to God for mercy, and God hears his prayers and takes his life. Reflecting back a few generations after Honi, a rabbi known to us only as Rava said, "Hence the saying 'Either companionship or death.'"

In one simple phrase, Rava has summarized one of the greatest plights of humanity, that of loneliness. Nearly everyone who has ever lived has experienced loneliness, a phenomenon that satirical novelist Joseph Heller once referred to as "the great plague" of human existence.[1] Loneliness is a feeling many of us know all too well. It is an existential longing for another. It is a deep desire for connection when there is none. To be lonely is to be spiritually and emotionally isolated. Loneliness is raw, human, and painful.

For Honi, his loneliness superseded all else. Schooled through his encounter at the carob tree that legacy and memory are central—the greatest tribute to the old gardener was that his grandson remembered that he planted the tree—he finds them lacking without companionship. Honi, who in a different tale was once saved from excommunication from the Jewish people because of his deep and profound relationship with God,[2] lacked that level of relationship with others. And for this reason, Honi chose not living over a life of loneliness.

For millennia, loneliness has been the subject of countless poems, books, songs, and works of art. Like Honi, many of the most indelible protagonists in history have suffered from it. It was the source of Holden Caulfield's angst and Gregor Samsa's depression; it drove Ethan Frome and Emma Bovary into the arms of another. Because of its proximity to art, there is beauty in the pain of these characters. They are interesting because of their isolation. Their suffering is a source of profundity.

In the first sentence of *Anna Karenina*, Leo Tolstoy writes, "All happy families are alike. Every unhappy family is unique in their unhappiness." In one single thought, Tolstoy sums up the fundamental fallacy about loneliness: if we want to be profound, we need to suffer in isolation. Happy families join other happy families in the mundanity of contentment. To truly stand out, we need to stand apart and alone from others.

Even when loneliness leads to trouble, as it did for Emma Bovary, who took her life at the end of *Madame Bovary*, or Gregor Samsa, who died alone in his parents' house covered in trash at the end of Franz Kafka's *The Metamorphosis*, we dismiss it. As the source and subject of these works, loneliness is a tool for our entertainment and enlightenment. It is a window into the psyche of these characters. True, we pause for a second to consider the destructive power of Bovary's or Samsa's loneliness, but that quickly fades as we admire the quality of prose and richness of mood created by their solitude.

Yet, as it was for Honi, there is little that is poetic and tragic about many of our lived experiences of loneliness. Honi's suffering was not beautiful or artful, just as ours is not. As a rabbi in Park Slope, Brooklyn, I have seen just how destructive and painful loneliness can be. People come to my office for any number of reasons, but they often share the fact that they are feeling profoundly alone. They live in a culture where they are constantly surrounded by people, yet their relationships are often proximal and superficial, and at the time when they need others the most, they feel their presence the least.

Some feel loneliness after losing a loved one. Mourning is a lonely enterprise. True, Jewish mourning rituals require that we fill our homes with community. Yet the true work of mourning, attempting to repair the gaping holes left in our hearts when a loved one leaves us, is often a solitary practice. Since every person's pain is a unique experience, it's often challenging to share it fully with others. We need time alone to heal, but all too often our friends forget to periodically check in after their initial outpouring of support.

For others, loneliness appears after the loss of a job. In Brooklyn today, we often ask immediately upon meeting someone new about their line of work. What could be a better way to quickly learn about

someone than finding out how they spend their days? Yet, for those facing unemployment, these questions can be devastating. Watching your
friends go to work when you struggle to find a job is lonely enough, but
these conversations only exacerbate the sense of solitude that comes
with job loss.

Others suffer because of the alienation of sickness. These are the
cries of the homebound and elderly who cannot leave their apart-
ments, or the adult child who must spend all his free time caring for
his aging parents. It is the young woman struggling with cancer when
her friends are healthy. It is the healthy couple who cannot conceive,
secretly visiting the fertility clinic, embarrassed to tell anyone of their
struggle.

Still others feel guilty for their loneliness. They are new parents
who feel blessed to have had a child but who feel alienated from the
outside world, confined to caring for a baby, a task that is simultaneously difficult and tedious. They yearn for adult conversation, worrying
if it's okay to be asking for a little separation this soon.

Some of my younger congregants are hit especially hard by how
easy it is to feel lonely in New York. For some in their twenties, it
has been years since the safety of college fostered and incubated new
friendships. It's easy to meet others when you are young. Yet, it seems
often impossible there. New York is a city of eight million people, yet
we struggle to find the courage to introduce ourselves to our neighbors
in the downstairs apartment.

I've watched others struggle with single life. Since the global match-
making industry is now a multibillion-dollar enterprise, it's impossible
to escape the reminders that you haven't found love. OkCupid and
JDate advertisements give the illusion that your life is forever lacking
without their aid. People become profiles, conversations become chats,
and we struggle to be seen amid the noise.

Conversely, others suffer in the depths of marriage. Many feel
invisible in their own home. Their lover's gaze that once looked into
them now looks through them. These congregants lack so much trust
in their relationship that they never know how their expressions of love
will be received. Then there is the loneliness of divorce, which comes

with its own host of fears: wondering which friends will remain by their side, needing to rebuild their social networks, or feeling the shame that others will judge them for giving up too soon.

I wrote this book for each of these individuals to help them deal with their shared experience of isolation and shame. While the book will not address each of their stories directly, it will aim to do something bigger. It will let them know that the Jewish tradition has much to say about loneliness. In the Hebrew Bible and Talmud, we have countless examples of loneliness. Personalities as diverse as Eve, Rachel, Aaron, Tzipporah, and King David have all faced loneliness, and learning their stories is the first step toward understanding that our struggles are not unique. Our ancestors are our companions in pain.

In fact, even the Jewish narrative of persecution and alienation can be used to help us understand that we are not alone in our suffering. But perhaps more powerful than any other voice, it is the "still small voice" of God's isolation that we must listen for. Indeed, if we are to understand that our solitude has a place in the universe, it is comforting to know that the Jewish tradition sees God as perhaps the loneliest of beings.

Yet, for as much comfort as it might bring to know that others have felt a similar suffering, it is only through deliberate community and companionship that we can truly feel less alone. While the first half of the book deals with empathetic voices in our sacred tradition, the second half deals with how we can be that comforting and open presence for others. It takes courage to cry out in our loneliness. How we respond when we hear another cry, both as an individual and as a community, may mean the difference between our efforts comforting another or further alienating them.

This book is an adaption of an ELI Talk that I gave on the topic of loneliness. At the time I first began to examine the topic, I was in the midst of a divorce. In one single season, as I moved from one session to the next of marriage counseling, I suddenly faced, for the first time ever, true loneliness. My shared social network was crumbling. My sense of self was called into question. I was unsure if the people who I had relied on for love and support would remain in my life.

Looking back, three things helped me get through this intense period of alienation. The first was the presence of good friends, who didn't try to solve my problems or show me pity. Instead these friends walked with me in my suffering and provided the greatest gift of all, their genuine presence. The second was my Jewish community. Coming to work every day and sharing in the joys and sorrows of my congregants gave purpose to my life and meaning to my suffering. I soon saw that my divorce was the first real trial of my adult life, and experiencing it helped me connect with the pain of others.

But perhaps more than anything else, the wisdom of my tradition gave me comfort. I could see myself in the stories of our ancient ancestors. Their struggles informed mine. The comforting words of our prophets and Rabbis supported me as much as any member of my social circle.

There is a powerful scene in the middle of D. H. Lawrence's novel *Lady Chatterley's Lover* when Mellors, the keeper of Lady Chatterley's family's estate and the object her affection, finds himself wandering outside of his mistress's property reflecting on his own loneliness:

> But he, the keeper, as the day grew, had realized: it's no good! It's no good trying to get rid of your own aloneness. You've got to stick to it all your life. Only at times, at times, the gap will be filled in. At times! But you have to wait for the times. Accept your own aloneness and stick to it, all your life. And then accept the times when the gap is filled in, when they come. But they've got to come. You can't force them.[3]

For Mellors (and for Lawrence), loneliness is a fundamental part of being human. It is our static state. At times we find reprieve, but these times cannot be controlled nor can they be predicted. To be human is to be fundamentally lonely. There is no remedy.

The purpose of this book is to challenge that notion and to ask what we can do in the face of loneliness to alleviate its harsh presence in our lives. As it did for me, our tradition, coupled with the thoughtfulness and compassion of intentional communities, can lift us from the

depths. Loneliness is not a permanent state. There is a way out of the
darkness. This book will help us find the right path.

A Note About Translations

Unless otherwise noted, all Bible translations are taken from the 1985
Jewish Publication Society translation. Most of the translations from
Talmud or Midrash are taken from the Soncino Press translations.
While I have kept many of the translations true to their source, I have
substituted the word "God" for "Lord" when applicable. In my commentary, I have attempted to limit the characterization of God as "He"
or "Him"; however, sometimes the rules of grammar have forced my
hand, and I have had to choose a pronoun. These should be taken not
as theological statements but rather as sacrifices toward the goal of
smoother prose.

PART 1

Understanding Loneliness

1

The Nature of Loneliness

What It Is, What It Isn't, and Why So Many of Us Are Lonely

Loneliness is the principal problem of human existence. It was there at the very beginning. Our yearning for companionship is part of the fabric of the universe, woven into being alongside the other miracles of God's hand.

In six days, God creates everything. Soon the skies are full of stars and birds, and the oceans teem with life. Plants sprout in every corner of the earth, and animals walk among them. At every stage, God calls this creation *tov*, "good." God is proud of the created universe. It is whole and beautiful.

To crown the achievement of creation, God creates humans. However, no sooner does God create humanity than God's attitude toward creation shifts. No longer is everything wonderful. As soon as we are created, God finds something that is not good.

Gazing upon Adam, God realizes an error. Quickly, God utters the first observation of the human condition: *Lo tov heyot ha'adam l'vado*, "It is not good for humanity to be alone" (Genesis 2:18). Writing thousands of years later, award-winning theologian Rabbi Steven Greenberg summarized God's statement: "The first fly in the ointment of creation is human loneliness."[1] At the moment of Adam's creation, God is surprised.

God had laid the world out for humanity's taking. Every plant, every animal was ours. Compared to all else, we were king. In fact, in one midrash we are told that God takes Adam around the garden saying, "Look at My works! See how beautiful they are—how excellent! For your sake I created them all" (*Ecclesiastes Rabbah* 7:3). Why, then, would we not be happy?

Yet with the whole garden before him, Adam is not content. In one particularly famous midrash, our Rabbis imagine God parading the animals in pairs before Adam. Two by two these creatures walk before him, waiting for a name. Adam names each animal, from the smallest to the largest. Yet no sooner does he finish his task than he turns to God, "Everyone has a partner, but I have none!" (*Genesis Rabbah* 17:4). Seeing Adam's pain, God knows it is time to create a companion for him.[2]

Through Eve's creation, Adam grew in a number of ways. Our Rabbis understood that Eve's birth symbolized the universal value of deep and meaningful relationships. With her by his side, they said, Adam would find many things: goodness, help, joy, blessing, atonement, and peace (*Genesis Rabbah* 17:2). Though the Rabbis were speaking of marriage, this ancient list is telling for what it teaches is missing in the absence of all powerful relationships like family, friends, coworkers, and community. Adam's loneliness made it impossible for him to achieve many of the foundational virtues of an actualized life. Without others in his life, Adam was empty. Without another to share his inner world he is described by the Rabbis as simply "flesh and blood" (*Pirke D'Rabbi Eliezer* 12). We need others to help us discover what is below the surface, to challenge us when we slip inward, and to probe our depths alongside us. If we are going to be joyful, if we going to be at peace, if we are to grow at all, we can't do it alone.

Connection—and Loneliness—Sustains Us

Our Rabbis were correct in listing Eve's effect on Adam. It's hard to feel happiness when we lack someone to share our joys with. It is impossible to feel centered when we have no one to comfort us and teach us we are safe. Life seems dulled when our eyes are the only ones observing the blessings around us. The perspective of others adds color to our world. Without confidence that others will answer, who can we cry out to for help in our time of need? Alone, the evils of the world seem sharper and more dangerous. And without others to turn to for forgiveness, it's much harder to feel better after we err. We need help to forgive ourselves in the face of a transgression. But if we feel we have no one, we must hold on to our deepest regrets and shame. There is no one to remind us that there can be an end to our guilt and remorse.

Eve's creation was meant to replace sorrow with joy, helplessness with support, unease with peace. In most cases, our closest loved ones do just that. In observing Adam's loneliness, God understood the profound role of others in our lives. Without our fellow human beings, we will never live life to its fullest, deepest, and highest. Turning toward others brings us face-to-face with connection. Their presence in our life is sustaining.

Because we need others to survive, it's no wonder that many scientists see loneliness as an important evolutionary tool to help us thrive. Though painful, loneliness is natural and it reminds us to seek out others when we become too far removed. In his book *Loneliness: Human Nature and the Need for Social Connection*, University of Chicago psychologist John Cacioppo notes that for our ancient ancestors living in the harsh realities of nature, a life lived apart was a life at risk.[3] As part of group, early humans had much more success fending off predators or doing the hard work of building shelters to keep safe from the elements. Loneliness is like physical pain; both serve to try to change our behavior. In the case of physical pain, our body reminds us to remove our hand from a fire or to rest after we have strained our muscles, to make sure that we do not become injured or deformed. Loneliness is psychological pain with a similar purpose. When we are lonely, our pain pushes us back toward community and into the safety and loving arms of others. Once we have returned to the group, we fall under their care, security, and support. Though there are certainly challenges when we deal with others—individuals can be cruel, callous, and opportunistic—evolution has proved that we are better off taking the risk of encountering those uncertainties than in going forward alone.

Loneliness, then, is the force that makes widowers seek out support, new parents register for infant music classes, divorcees pursue love again, and recent urban transplants join sports leagues. Loneliness is the engine of connection. Because of Adam's loneliness, he found companionship. Because of ours, we find others.

Not All Loneliness Is Alike

The world we live in is much more complex than that of our ancestors, and loneliness comes with its risks. Studies have shown that there are two types of loneliness. The first, known as temporal loneliness, is short-term and situation specific. We all experience this type of loneliness many times in a given year. It is triggered by a big move, a new job, or the loss of a relationship. Our loneliness is tied directly to our circumstances. We are lonely *because of something*. The answer to this loneliness is to remove its source or replace it with another person or activity. Often this works. New relationships help us deal with old ones. After switching jobs, time allows us the opportunity to make connections with our coworkers. We get up the courage to knock on our neighbor's door and we know we have a friendly face in the hallways. Temporal loneliness is challenging but not overwhelming. Yes, it hurts a bit and seems daunting, but we trust it is not permanent. We encounter it with the spirit that King Solomon penned his famous adage *Gam zeh yaavor*, "This too shall pass."[4]

Yet for many, this temporal loneliness can, over time, turn into a chronic loneliness from which escape is much harder. Scientists are not entirely sure why some people are more prone to lifelong struggles with loneliness. They suspect that it has to do with the same evolutionary processes that brought about loneliness in the first place. Evolution is a precarious balancing act. Certain species of bird, for example, need large feathers to attract mates; however, if their feathers get too big, they become slow and subject to predators. Physical pain works the same way. Too little pain allows us the ability to take unnecessary risks, causing broken bones and infection. But too much pain can cripple us and ruin our lives.

Loneliness embodies the same tension. Too little loneliness may cause us to venture for too long in the wilderness, but too much causes us to suffer in a wholly different way. Like physical pain, there are some people who feel it more acutely than others. The same stubbed toe in one person may elicit a wince, while for another it causes a full-throated cry. Often when we see different reactions to pain, we assume that one person is simply more expressive and attention seeking than another. However, this is far from the truth. The same painful stimulus is felt along a continuum. Working in the same way, the same divorce or cross-country relocation may affect two people in completely different ways. For one, the pain will always remain temporal and the cause benign. This first group can tolerate solitude and isolation and can see a way out. They hunger less for companionship, just as some hunger less for food. It's in their DNA not to need others as much. Being comfortable alone doesn't mean they disappear from society. It simply means if they happen to find themselves away from it, they do not hurt.

For others, however, even a trigger that society deems as small, like a fight with a friend or the loss of a pet, may quickly develop into a kind of loneliness that seems incurable and acute. Those who are in it feel trapped. They do not feel seen by others. In their loneliness, they feel invisible. There are many descriptions in our tradition of this experience, but perhaps the most profound sentiment of the hopelessness of alienation appears in Psalm 41:6–10:

> My enemies speak evilly of me,
>> "When will he die and his name perish?"
> If one comes to visit, he speaks falsely;
>> his mind stores up evil thoughts;
>> once outside, he speaks them.
> All my enemies whisper together against me,
>> imagining the worst for me.
>> "Something baneful has settled in him;
>> he'll not rise from his bed again."
> My ally in whom I trusted,
>> even he who shares my bread,
>> has been utterly false to me.

The author of this psalm thinks that he has no one. Because it is written in the first person, it is difficult to know whether the torment and persecution expressed in the poem are real. It is almost too grotesque to believe. However, the psalms are profound not because they are accurate. They are powerful because they are true to the human experience. The author's experience of alienation is authentic to him, and it is tragic and painful. Loneliness is real for those who suffer it, and denying that will only further deepen its effect.

Though extremely particular to the psalmist's experience, there are elements of this psalm that speak to the universal experience of chronic loneliness. Many who are suffering from loneliness feel their friends have abandoned them. Those with whom they used to share their bread have turned away, showing falsehoods rather than engaging with genuine connection. Like the author, some wonder how many others would care if they disappeared. They wonder if their presence matters and if anyone notices them. Still others internalize the message given to the author by his enemies; when we are truly and profoundly lonely, it is nearly impossible to find our way out. We are afflicted by a "baneful" disease, and we wonder if we will ever get up from where we lie.

The Dangers of Loneliness

There is little question from this psalm that the social pain depicted in these words puts the author at risk for other, more serious issues. In addition to reading alienation, isolation, and desolation from his words of loneliness, it's also not hard to imagine that the psalmist suffers from depression, anxiety, paranoia, and self-loathing.

Loneliness is dangerous. It can affect concentration and the ability to create and store new memories. It can also make it hard to sleep or hard to awaken. Studies have shown that lonely individuals are more likely to take their own lives.[5] Other studies explain that chronically lonely individuals have lower functioning immune systems[6] and higher rates of heart disease.[7] In fact, one recent article explained that loneliness is as dangerous to our health as obesity and that the effects of loneliness on our bodies are equal to being a chronic alcoholic or smoking fifteen cigarettes a day."[8]

In the era well before science proved the risks of loneliness, the Rabbis described its destruction. According to Midrash, the worst of the ten plagues in Egypt was not the death of the firstborn but rather the plague of darkness (*Exodus Rabbah* 14:14). The darkness that fell over Egypt was so thick that no one could interact with another. Not only could they not see, but they could not hear or speak. In fact, according to some commentators, the darkness was so thick that they could not move. Paralyzed and isolated, many thousands perished, perhaps more than during the final plague.

Loneliness can also affect our higher-level brain functions.[9] It impairs our ability to solve problems, regulate our behavior, and attain perspective. Ironically, the part of the brain affected by loneliness is the exact part that we need to employ when we seek to find a way out of our loneliness. If we are less able to devise solutions to our loneliness, summon willpower to leave our homes and enter into the world, and see our loneliness as temporary, it becomes much harder to believe we can improve. Because of this, chronic loneliness tends to be self-perpetuating and hard to escape.

The Pervasiveness of Our Suffering

Today more than perhaps at any other time in recent memory, so many are struggling with chronic loneliness. A recent study by the Church Urban Fund and the Church of England found that between 2012 and 2015, there was a 10 percent jump in clergy reporting that loneliness was a major problem among their congregants.[10] Another report by the National Science Foundation found that "unprecedented numbers of Americans are lonely." Writing about the report in the *American Spectator*, Janice Shaw Crouse explains:

> The study featured 1,500 face-to-face interviews where more than a quarter of the respondents—one in four— said that they have no one with whom they can talk about their personal troubles or triumphs. If family members are not counted, the number doubles to more than half of Americans who have no one outside their immediate family with whom they can share confidences. Sadly, the researchers noted increases in "social

isolation" and "a very significant decrease in social connection to close friends and family."[11]

There is no easy answer to why so many today are suffering. For
some it might be because of the breakdown of social structures. In
his book *Bowling Alone*, Robert D. Putnam explains that today as many
people as ever are bowling but fewer than ever are joining bowling leagues.[12] In other words, a record number of people are bowling by themselves. Using this phenomenon as a metaphor, Putnam
examines the decline of the institutions that held us together. These
include participation in religious institutions like synagogues and
churches, civil institutions like the PTA, volunteer institutions like
the Red Cross, and even family institutions. Compared to the 1960s,
families have 60 percent fewer family picnics and 40 percent fewer
family dinners.[13]

Putnam's research highlights an important trend in the Jewish
community: the rise of the "sovereign self," a term coined by Steven
M. Cohen and Arnold M. Eisen.[14] Throughout their book *The Jew
Within*, Cohen and Eisen point to an important change in the way we
relate to our Judaism; we have made a turn inward toward meaning
making and identity building.[15] Today, members of the Jewish community often privilege the personal over the collective. These Jews,
of which I am one, desire autonomy. They understand that others
have much to teach but the ultimate arbiter is the self. Their inner
life and inner growth are paramount. Though they see themselves
as part of a people, their sense of belonging is ancillary to their own
journeys.

This trend shouldn't be surprising; already in the 1970s Tom Wolfe
dubbed the baby boomers the "me generation." Since then, subsequent
generations have adopted that distinction. A somewhat recent cover
story by *Time* magazine termed the millennials the "me me me generation."[16] Much good can come from focusing inward; it leads to introspection, meaning making, and self-discovery. Yet, too much emphasis
on the personal has eroded the bonds that hold our community together.
Loneliness is the consequence of the self, run amok.

So Many "Friends," Still Lonely

In addition to the rise of the individual, there are many other reasons why loneliness has emerged so strongly in recent years. Technology, for example, connects us quickly to the farthest corners of the earth; however, it fails in one fundamental way: many of its platforms are inherently impersonal. There is a hierarchy of interactions. The deepest communication happens when we can use all our senses to convey our thoughts. In person, we hear another's tone, sense their energy, and see their expressions. Our phone takes away sight; text takes away voice. Even video falls short; a surprising amount of information is conveyed by smell. But more than all of these, social media lacks the most engagement. A "like" will never be an embrace, a "re-tweet" never a smile. Technology has increased our number of cyber acquaintances while masking our diminishing friendships. A recent study found that 48 percent of respondents today only had one confidant, whereas in a similar study twenty-five years ago the average number was three.[17] This is despite the fact that many of us have upward of a thousand "friends" or "followers."

Technology also serves as a reinforcement to the fallacy that others have it better than we do. Most people are very careful about what they put online. We cultivate an image and groom a persona. We won't show the world the three weekends we spend alone, only the one where we are with our friends. We all know that social media is curated, but it's easy to forget this when we log onto the computer and see only happy and smiling faces. Facebook shows us the five friends who got married, not the ten who are struggling with single life. We see pictures of many babies but hear very few stories of infertility. Social media drives us toward loneliness and then reminds us why we are there in the first place.

Today we live our lives "alone together," a term coined by Sherry Turkle to describe the phenomenon of people being with one another while simultaneously being elsewhere.[18] We all know this process well. How many of us have texted while in an important meeting or checked Facebook at the dinner table? In Turkle's words:

> People want to customize their lives. They want to go
> in and out of all the places they are, because the thing
> that matters most to them is control over where they
> put their attention.... People can't get enough of each
> other, if and only if they have each other at a distance,
> in amounts they can control.[19]

The problem with these kinds of interactions is that they leave others powerless.

One of the fundamental ways we can let others know that they matter is by conveying to them that we will drop everything if they reach out to us. We give them power by allowing them to take our attention. However, if we communicate to others that when they call we *might* listen or that we would rather rush to our phones than to their side, it sends the message that they are a low priority and their presence in our lives does not matter.

Solitude versus Loneliness

Reflecting further, Turkle cites the lack of solitary spaces as a reason for why we are so isolated. Being alone is not the same thing as being lonely. In fact, there is tremendous value in taking time away from others. For many, being alone provides space for creativity and self-reflection. Writers, artists, hikers, and gurus all spend a great deal of time alone. Being alone helps us better understand ourselves, providing us space for introspection. I have had many conversations with congregants who love to travel alone. They find it empowering and centering. Our busy lives often leave little room to reconnect with the self. Being alone creates the space to revisit the soul. This may be why Henry David Thoreau once called solitude his greatest "companion."[20]

Rebbe Nachman of Breslov knew well the power of being alone. Nachman prescribed that we should all spend time alone in the wilderness, communing and literally speaking with God in a process known as *hitbodedut*. By going out alone into nature, Nachman would find comfort and holiness in solitude. Reflecting on this process, Nachman famously wrote:

Grant me the ability to be alone;
>   may it be my custom to go outdoors each day
>   among the trees and grass—among all growing things
>   and there may I be alone, and enter into prayer,
>   to talk with the One to whom I belong.
May I express there everything in my heart,
>   and may all the foliage of the field—
>   all grasses, trees, and plants—
>   awake at my coming,
>   to send the powers of their life into the words of my prayer
>   so that my prayer and speech are made whole
>   through the life and spirit of all growing things,
>   which are made as one by their transcendent Source.
May I then pour out the words of my heart
>   before Your Presence like water, O God,
>   and lift up my hands to You in worship,
>   on my behalf, and that of children![21]

Nachman, who struggled with depression and often felt lonely throughout his life, ironically did not feel lonely when alone. In nature he felt close to God. In fact, in one of his writings he imagined that nature itself accompanied him in times of solitude: "As often as you can, take a trip out to the fields to pray. All the grasses will join you. They will enter your prayers and give you strength to sing praises to God."[22] Rebbe Nachman is a wonderful example of how to use loneliness for good, and we will revisit him in this book.

The problem today is that we often confuse aloneness and loneliness. We are so worried that if we are alone, we will become lonely. We are so afraid to be alone that participants in one recent study preferred delivering electric shocks to themselves rather than spend time alone in a room for fifteen minutes.[23] We are anxious about being alone because solitude needs nurturing. It is a muscle and it can atrophy. If we distract ourselves and never learn to embrace aloneness, the only option is to feel lonely when these distractions are not available.

Lonely in Plain Sight

If being alone does not lead always to loneliness, then loneliness too is felt not only when we are alone. We can actually feel lonely in the most crowded of places. Loneliness can appear when we are on a subway during rush hour, in religious services, and lying beside a loved one. In fact, the anonymity of crowds may be a huge factor in why so many in large cities feel lonely. We are so often surrounded by people, but they are not our community. They do not see us. They barely notice us. I, like many in my congregation, have observed a person crying on the train and said nothing. Proximity is not the same thing as presence.

Rebbe Nachman, who so loved his time alone with nature, also felt alienated among groups of his disciples. In his biography of Nachman, Arthur Green observed that when surrounded by his students, Nachman would feel the most alone. He would fade into himself, saying, "When everyone is standing around me and I am seated in their midst—that is when I practice *hitbodedut*."[24] Remarking on Nachman's struggle, Green writes:

> The picture emerges of a hidden and lonely figure, surrounded by admirers who occasionally merit to be told how little they understand who he really is. The child who seeks a lone path to God, apparently not pleased by the attention or companionship of others, grows into the adult who knows that he is deeply alone, even in the midst of the admiring crowd.[25]

For Nachman, as for us, attention does nothing to help us overcome our loneliness. If we feel invisible, if we feel that others do not care about the real us, it does not matter how many people are around. Literature abounds with examples of public displays of loneliness. I've always felt for F. Scott Fitzgerald's Gatsby, who despite his standing in the community and his many "friends" still feels lonely after hosting them at his house. After one such party, we read of Gatsby, "a sudden emptiness seemed to flow now from the windows and the great doors, endowing with complete isolation the figure of the host, who stood on the porch, his hand up in a formal gesture of farewell."[26]

Both Gatsby and Nachman express a phenomenon seen by our Rabbis in their description of a gathering that once took place in Jerusalem. The Rabbis say that when gathered together at the Temple, the pilgrims stood pressed together; yet when they bowed toward God, each had ample room: "Rabbi Samuel bar Rabbi Jonah said: Each had four cubits, a cubit on each side, so that none should hear his neighbor's prayer" (*Genesis Rabbah* 5:7). Many know this feeling. We are in a group, but suddenly it seems as if there is a bubble around us. As close as others may get, they will never enter. We are shouting into the ether and no one notices. Loneliness disappears when others hear our prayer, not when they are deaf to it.

The Driving Forces of Loneliness

Rabbi Joseph B. Soloveitchik understood this well. In his book *The Lonely Man of Faith*, he points out that there is no easy answer to the problem of loneliness. The reason that alleviating loneliness is so difficult is because our first instinct to deal with the problem may actually make the problem worse. In his book, Soloveitchik explains that we have two forces within us, which he calls the "majestic man" and the "covenantal man."[27] The first force seeks fulfillment through conquering the world. This is our impulse to build large buildings and explore the universe. It is our impulse to embrace science and power. It is also the high we get when we work a room, make business connections, or add an important perspective to a discussion. Our majestic impulse is fulfilled through mastery, ownership, and achievement.

The problem today is that our majestic force does little to help our loneliness. We can't build our loneliness away, nor can we master it. Money and power cannot buy happiness. In fact, becoming great can make us more lonely; to achieve great things, many choose or are forced to alienate others. Many people climb the social ladder by stepping on those beneath them. Others, like great artists, sacrifice relationships and seclude themselves to make space to create.

Yet, too often, we feel the need to feed the majestic part of ourselves in an attempt to alleviate loneliness even though we know implicitly that doing so is futile. We don't get along with our coworkers, so we assume that if we only succeeded more, then they would like us. We have problems at home and we think that more money will solve our marital difficulties. We move to a new city and hope that signing up for a club or team will bring us friends.

The Jewish community often buys into these fallacies. Increasing attendance at services is not the answer to our congregants' loneliness. More lectures and programs will give our community more ways to spend their time but will not make them feel more seen and loved. If we are going to help those who are lonely in our midst find comfort and companionship, we can't solve it though majestic capacities.

Instead, we need to feed the other, covenantal part of our soul. Rather than being fed by achievement, our covenantal impulse seeks deeper connection with others and God. This part of ourselves wants purpose over accomplishment, presence over power, love over gain. The covenantal person is the embodiment of our chronic loneliness and cannot be fed by the simple delights of living in the world. Popularity is irrelevant. Our covenantal selves want to really be seen by others as we engage in deeply meaningful, reciprocal relationships.

In the book of Ecclesiastes we read about the importance of nurturing our covenantal spirit. Beginning by examining the folly of the majestic self, the author writes, "And I have noted this further futility under the sun: the case of the man who is alone, with no companion, who has neither son nor brother; yet he amasses wealth without limit and his eye is never sated with riches.... That too is a futility and an unhappy business" (Ecclesiastes 4:7–8). However, no sooner does the author condemn the search for riches and prestige than he explains the value of connection: "Two are better off than one.... For should they fall, one can raise the other" (Ecclesiastes 4:9–10). Here, the answer to loneliness is found in reaching outward. The salve for our broken souls is love.

The rest of this book is an answer to the cry of our covenantal selves. There is no easy answer to the problem of loneliness in our lives. If there was, we would have found it already. The world is too complex and the reasons for our isolation too varied for platitudes. There are four ways we can reach when yearning for connection: out, up, in, and back. Later in the book we will examine the first three. We deal with loneliness by reaching out to others, up to God, and in toward ourselves. But first, it is helpful to look back toward the suffering and alienation of our ancestors. Through their stories we may see our own. We may learn from their struggles and follies. But more than anything, their loneliness might become a mirror in which to see our suffering, and through them we may find a companion in our pain.

2

The Loneliness of Love

Finding, Keeping, and Losing It

The Loneliness of Single Life

Although dating today has no perfect parallel in our classical Jewish cast of characters, the biblical Tamar (Genesis 38) embodies much of the loneliness that comes with modern single life.

In her effort to find love, Tamar faces constant roadblocks. According to the biblical account, Tamar marries a man named Er, who was the son of Judah, one of Jacob's sons and the brother of Joseph. Quickly after the wedding Er is put to death by God. Tamar then is given Er's brother Onan as a husband. However, he too sins and then dies. Ready to marry again, Tamar awaits Judah's promise of his third and youngest son, Shelah.

The longer Tamar waits for this promise to come true, however, the less she believes it ever will. Judah has no intention of giving her his final son. Tamar is tainted. She is what later commentators would call a *katalanit*, a husband killer.[1] Seeing how scared Judah is to give his final son to her, we can't help but imagine how his inaction might affect Tamar's self-worth, perhaps leading her to feel that she is unworthy of love. She has lost her previous two chances at happiness, through no fault of her own, but is somehow implicated. Judah's message is loud and clear: their death is her shame.

Tamar's shame today is still present. Finding love can throw into question the fundamental things we believe about ourselves. It's easy to feel defective when others do not respond to us. Modern dating is a dance. We reveal a piece of ourselves in the hopes of seeing a piece of another. Naturally, many dances end. By no fault of hers, Tamar cannot find stability. When her dances end, she is left with only questions. Relationships are complex things. There are too many factors involved to explain truly why some succeed and some fail. An odd array of circumstances lead her to move from Er to Onan to the promise of Shelah, and like modern romance, each relationship is unique. She, however, is the common denominator, and like all of us, when faced with failure she turns inward and risks blaming herself.

Our Invisible Virtues

Our tradition sees Tamar as so much more than her quest for love. According to Rabbinic lore, Tamar is a rich and fascinating character who should not be defined solely by the men she pursues. Some accounts mention that Tamar grows up an orphan. Overcoming great odds, Tamar perseveres. She meets her husband, converts to Judaism, and seeks the family that she lacked as a child (Talmud, *Sotah* 10a). Other accounts see her story as the opposite. Instead of overcoming a challenging past, she abandons a privileged one. She is the daughter of Melchizedek, the king of Salem.[2] Her story is one of humility. She leaves a pampered existence to find love (*Genesis Rabbah* 85:10).

Whatever the story, Tamar's past is important because it shows her character. I often meet with couples before their wedding and ask them what they observed on their first date that made them continue seeing one another. Some say they liked the ease of the interaction, others say they felt attraction, but more often than not couples continue because they see depth in the other person. Though they cannot define exactly what is underneath because it is too early to tell, they are nevertheless intrigued. Usually, these early kernels appear again later when I ask in our final meeting, "What do you love today about your partner?" By now, the glimpses they got early on have become the foundations for what they love and what will sustain their relationship for years to come.

Part of the reason that dating is lonely is because we know that we have something to offer. Like Tamar, we may be proud of our courage and perseverance, our humility and strength, all of which are found in her story. Or we might pride ourselves on our determination, our compassion, our warmth, and our optimism. More often than not, we meet others who are blind to these virtues. Not everyone appreciates us as our future husband or wife will.

When we date, there are usually two reasons why someone does not acknowledge our gifts: they may not value them enough to notice, or less frequently, we have not fully conveyed them. However, we often add a third reason. Perhaps the virtues we are most proud of do not exist at all. Perhaps we are not as nurturing, open, and thoughtful as we think, and this only alienates us from ourselves, moving us toward loneliness. However, even if we are able to see the first two reasons, there are risks. If we cannot convey the things for which we are proudest, we start labeling ourselves as "bad daters." This attitude promotes anxiety and frustration. We know we are lovable, we know we have gifts, but, we say, because of our nerves or shyness or insecurity, no one will ever know.

Sadly, the argument that we haven't found someone who appreciates our gifts is surprisingly insidious and perhaps the most troubling of all. If we think we are worthy of another's love but cannot find that person, it is only natural to assume that there is no one out there. We are raised with the conception of the soul mate, the *beshert*, a certain person who is our perfect complement. The Talmud tells us that this match is divinely ordained forty days before conception (*Sotah* 2a). In fact, in one teaching by Nachmanides, we are said to be incomplete without the other.[3] Nachmanides writes that before birth our souls are full. Before sending them down to us, God cuts these souls in half, sending each down into a different body. The quest for love is the act of one soul looking for its mate, yearning to be whole again. Our *beshert* then is the one who sees our gifts. But the longer we wait, the more we doubt he or she exists. Maybe God forgot to send my other half? Maybe the story is wrong? If there is no one for us in the world, the natural reaction is a profound feeling of isolation.

Hiding from Our True Selves

There is, however, another tragedy inherent in Tamar's story that is also central to the plight of single life. Tamar has a history, one worthy of sharing. Whichever narrative we believe—that she came from nothing or left everything behind—the Torah does not communicate it. It leaves out her past. We know this only because the Rabbis chose to share it. The only thing we know about Tamar, her whole life in fact, is wrapped up in one single quest: to find a stable husband and produce a family. Her values and virtues, her dignity and strength, are secondary to this pursuit. I've talked to too many wonderful people in my congregation who all bemoan the same injustice. They say, "I've done everything I want in life. I have a career, an education, great friendships, and strong values. The only thing I am missing is love, and this seems to be the measure by which I'm judged by myself and others." When we struggle to achieve a dream, it looms large and overshadows everything else we have accomplished. This happens with every perceived failure, but because finding love is so connected to our sense of self, this struggle casts a particularly large shadow.

Eventually, Tamar's struggle reaches a climax. The narrative continues. Tamar learns that her father-in-law Judah is coming to Timnah, where Tamar is residing. Hearing this, Tamar takes off her widow's clothes, covers herself with a veil, and sits down along the road to Timnah in a place called Petach Enaim.

The act of taking off her widow's clothing and donning a veil is important to understanding Tamar's mind-set at the time. Throughout the book of Genesis, many women have worn veils, and each time this small piece of cloth has symbolized hiding. Earlier in the book of Genesis, Rebekah falls off her camel when meeting her future husband Isaac for the first time. Looking up at him, she exclaims with exuberance, "Who is that guy!" Yet, no sooner does she let out her burst of emotion than she backtracks. She puts on a veil and hides beneath it, ashamed of having become overexcited by Isaac.

Like Rebekah, Leah too dons a veil. Students of Torah will remember that our patriarch Jacob immediately falls in love with Leah's younger sister Rachel when they first meet. Seeking to marry her, Jacob strikes a deal with her father Laban: he will work seven years and afterward gain her hand in marriage. However, on the wedding night, Laban switches daughters. Under a veil, hiding her identity, Leah marries Jacob. The veil allows her to imitate Rachel, to bury her own personhood and assume that of another.

Tamar's veil serves a similar purpose. Like Rebekah and Leah before her, Tamar hides under it. Tamar will play the harlot. Abandoning her widow's clothing and donning her veil, Tamar leaves behind her true self. For the afternoon, Tamar will no longer be Judah's daughter-in-law. Instead, she becomes a seductress. She seduces Judah in the hopes of becoming pregnant with his child and becoming a mother through him, a task in which she ultimately succeeds.

Though certainly an extreme case, Tamar's story is one very familiar to those struggling to find love. Tamar believes that the only way to succeed in building her family is to hide herself and pretend to be another. Though Tamar has no alternative to this—societal norms dictate that she will be stuck waiting for a husband who will never be hers—we certainly have a choice today. I've seen too many friends pretend to be someone other than who they are for someone else. If someone does not love us for our passions, our virtues, and our beliefs, they do not deserve our love. How many of us have hidden the best of ourselves, placing a veil before us, because the thought of living alone is more frightening than the thought of changing who we are?

I've always loved the scene in the movie *Runaway Bride* where Ike, Richard Gere's character, confronts Maggie Carpenter, Julia Roberts's character, about her veil. Gere plays a journalist who is researching why Roberts consistently abandons her lovers at the altar—she has run away three times and is about to do it a fourth. He discovers that the reason she flees is that Roberts becomes whoever her fiancé wants her to be and at the last minute panics that she has lost herself. In one climactic scene, Gere points out her folly through the metaphor of the eggs she ate in her previous relationships: "With the priest, you liked them scrambled. With the Dead Head, fried. With the bug guy, poached. Now it's egg whites."

Like many of us, Roberts's character wants to be loved. She also has fears: fear of rejection and fear of being alone. Because she is afraid, she hides her fears by trying on the persona of another. Then, she realizes too late that she has tricked her husband-to-be into loving someone else. They love someone who looks like her but is not her at all. Changing who you are creates alienation from self and resentment toward the other who may not even know that by embracing your veil, they have implicitly rejected your person.

As unhealthy as Tamar may have been by placing the veil on herself, I have always admired one thing she does during her time in Petach Enaim. The medieval mystics imagine that the place name, literally "the opened eyes," is a physical description of the tent in which Tamar was sitting (*Zohar* 3:71b). In their imagination, Tamar opens up each flap so that the tent is open on all sides. Though they understand this as connecting to the biblical Abraham, who proved his virtue and hospitality by opening his tent to all who passed by, there is something much more profound in Tamar's act.

A fully open tent resembles perfectly a chuppah, a wedding canopy, open in all directions.[4] At the moment of turning away from her dreams, minutes before heading out to seduce her father-in-law as a final effort to gain a family, Tamar gives herself the wedding she has sought. Her veil becomes bridal, her tent holy. This single act is perhaps the most tragic part of the story but also the most cathartic. In opening up her tent, Tamar is saying, "I know my future will not turn out how I wanted so I'm mourning that vision, and when I am ready, I will walk out toward a new one."

Mourning What Was, Shaping What Can Be

One of the hardest parts of single life is knowing that our vision of the future is not solely in our hands. I've talked to many people who have had a timeline of when they wanted to marry, when they wanted have children, and how they wanted to grow old. The harder it is for us to adapt our vision and the more we hold on to it in the face of failure, the more alienated we feel.

Tamar's story is tragic because it reminds us of what is hard about being single—the shame, the hiding, the questioning, and the powerlessness—but it does teach us one affirming lesson: if we allow ourselves to fully mourn our timelines, we can rewrite them. Tamar's path to motherhood is unorthodox. Today, no one would seduce their father-in-law to become a parent. However, in being able to reimagine her future, in knowing that even if it's not exactly what she expected, she is able to create one that is both powerful and joyful. Tamar makes space for what is to come by allowing herself to grieve over what she thought might be. And in the end, Tamar is happy. Rabbinic tradition explains that her children are righteous, and she is good mother (*Genesis Rabbah* 85:13). And in a wonderful irony, perhaps because of her willingness to let go, Tamar becomes a foremother of King David and one day the ancestor to the Messiah.

The Loneliness in Marriage

While there are countless examples in Jewish literature of both women and men stuck in loveless or unhealthy marriages, the marriage between Adam and Eve is particularly tragic. Although Christian and Jewish scholars alike have condemned Eve for eating from the Tree of Knowledge of Good and Evil and bringing about humanity's exile from the Garden of Eden, there are a number of stories that see her part in our saga as extremely tragic. For, throughout her life, Eve struggled a great deal with feeling loved by her husband Adam.

There is an ancient belief that Eve was not her husband's first love. According to Rabbinic lore, God first assigns Adam a wife named Lilith, who was equal to Adam in every way (*Alphabet of Ben Sira* 78). When Adam tests that equality, however, demanding that Lilith submit to him in the bedroom, she runs away. Refusing to come back even when asked by three of God's angels, she marries the "great demon," a devil-like figure in the Jewish tradition known later as Samael.

Burdened by Baggage

It is not always easy to be with someone who has a storied history with another. It's an all-too-familiar fact that with any partner, you enter into a conversation about love and commitment that was begun by another but that you must continue. If we have ever loved before, then we have baggage from that relationship. Sometimes, these previous experiences make us stronger, better husbands or wives. At other times, however, they burden us with fear, anxiety, and anger, all of which can make us guarded and distant.

Knowing that Adam is already upset about his first marriage and fearing that he will not get along with his next wife, God puts measures in place to ensure Adam will value Eve. According to the midrash cited in the previous chapter, the reason God parades the animals in couples before Adam is to stir in him the desire for a true partner (*Genesis Rabbah* 17:4). And it works for a while. Adam and Eve's wedding is considered one of the greatest in the history of humankind (*Midrash Psalms* 68:4). For the ceremony, God personally dresses Eve in the greatest jewelry of creation (*Genesis Rabbah* 18:3). God then braids her hair and escorts her to Adam (Talmud, *Berachot* 61a). Even their chuppah is special. While grooms traditionally have one chuppah and kings have three, Adam and Eve are given ten (*Sefer Hazikronot* 7:1–2).

However, the seeds planted by Adam's past do not take long to sprout. Perhaps the greatest challenge of any relationship is that time changes people. In the words of French author Pamela Druckerman, "People's youthful quirks can harden into adult pathologies. What's adorable at 20 can be worrisome at 30 and dangerous at 40."[5] Ignoring behaviors does not make them go away. Instead habits form and ruts develop. Our tradition understood this and taught in a somewhat crude metaphor that a dog that is allowed to eat its own sick will inevitably learn to develop a taste for it (Talmud, *Yoma* 86b, based on Proverbs 26:11).

Suffering in Second Place

Like every relationship, Adam and Eve's marriage has its stressors that creep between them and habits that drive them apart. Ironically, God becomes one of the great wedges in their marriage. According to one account of their wedding, God is Adam's best man (Talmud, *Eruvin* 18a). After the wedding, God continues to privilege Adam. Adam would recline in Eden while ministering angels hovered over him, roasting flesh and straining wine for him (Talmud, *Sanhedrin* 59b). Created to be Adam's companion, Eve finds herself in a triangle. Adam's true attention and love is directed toward heaven. With no other place to turn, the young bride finds her marriage defined by incredible solitude and isolation.

Many know Eve's feeling. We want to know that those to whom we are married privilege us above all else. The times that are the loneliest in marriage are when our paramount status is superseded by another person or thing. It's natural that for Adam, this thing is God—God was, after all, there with Adam from the start. But work, hobbies, and commitments can also drive a wedge between two people. Anything or anyone that conveys the message "You are not my deepest passion" acts as an alienating force on a wanting partner.

There is an ancient debate that speaks to Eve's loneliness in her secondary status. Asking the question "Where was Adam during the hours when Eve ate the forbidden fruit?" a midrash gives us two equally troubling answers:

> Abba bar Guria said: He had engaged in intercourse and had fallen asleep. But the sages said: At that time, the Holy One was taking him around the entire world, saying to him: Here is a place fit for planting trees, here is a place fit for sowing cereals. (*Genesis Rabbah* 19:3)

Neither answer paints a particularly flattering picture of Adam. Both stories show that in addition to God, Adam finds other projects that distance him from his wife. The sages see his pursuit as one of livelihood; Adam is off getting fulfillment without Eve, with his work of planting and tending to the garden. Abba bar Guria has a much harsher critique, however. Adam is the stereotypical distant lover, who after intercourse would rather nap than engage with Eve. For Adam, sex is less a path to intimacy and connection and more a means toward a pleasurable end. When he is done, he has little use for his wife. Both work and sex are important in a marriage—work provides funds to live off of and sex creates bonds—but when they become more important than the marriage itself, loneliness follows.

The Blame Game

Sadly, fighting about these behaviors doesn't always work. Using the same metaphor of the dog, our Rabbis condemn those who engage in the cycle of sinning and apologizing, sinning and apologizing (Talmud, *Yoma* 86b). Arguments can become productive or they can become routine. When they are productive, they lead to listening and changes in behavior. When they are routine, we learn exactly how to have them, what to say and how to act, but then return to the same behavior with little result. They become rituals that do little more than mark time in our relationships. When arguments lose their weight and influence, we often feel that our main tool to express our discontent has been exhausted and we have no other means through which to be heard.

Eventually, Eve eats the forbidden fruit from the Tree of Knowledge of Good and Evil, causing exile from the garden. This act only widens the gap between husband and wife. In one of the most tragic scenes of their relationship, Adam disavows himself of his connection to his wife at the moment of crisis. After he and Eve share in the forbidden fruit, he criticizes God in his wife's presence: "The woman *You put at my side*—she gave me of the tree, and I ate" (Genesis 3:12). Adam's use of pronouns is glaring. "You gave Eve to me. I had no choice in the matter. And now I'm being punished on her behalf?" Soon after blaming Eve for tricking him into eating the fruit, Adam vows to avoid Eve altogether so as not to bring a child into a world where he or she is destined to die—death was the punishment brought on humanity after the two were expelled from the garden. According to Midrash, however, God shows Adam that after twenty-six generations, Israel will stand at the foot of Mount Sinai and accept the Torah, and he feels comforted with the future and returns to his wife (*Genesis Rabbah* 21:9).

Here Adam is unpredictable. In her book *All Joy and No Fun*, critic and writer Jennifer Senior explains that one of the great predictors of happiness is "flow." She writes, "Flow is a state of being in which we are so engrossed in the task at hand—so fortified by our own sense of agency, of mastery—that we lose all sense of our surroundings, as though time has stopped."[6] For many, the act of being in a productive marriage can increase the sense of flow; we have a partner who is by our side and facilitates our agency and mastery. But when marriages are unpredictable and unhealthy, they inhibit flow, taking us away from being present in our relationship because we are always wondering what curveball will come next.

The Dangers of Distraction

Soon after her husband's abandonment and return, Eve gives birth to Cain and Abel. For her, these two children are miracles, and they are also rich with possibility. Not only will they be better companions to her than Adam, but they might also provide a platform for renewed commitment with her husband. When her son Cain is born, Eve proclaims, "With God's help, I have acquired a man" (Genesis 4:1, translation mine). Though the plain meaning for the verse is "With God's help, I have acquired a male child," the Rabbis play with the word *kaniti* (I have acquired), which can also mean "I have betrothed." They read her cry as saying, "With God's help, I have renewed my vows with my man [i.e., Adam]." In other words, after struggling with Adam's acceptance in the Garden of Eden and his distance after their expulsion, Eve sees the birth of her child as the remedy for their broken relationship.

But as we know, having a child together is perhaps the worst way to try to fix a failing marriage. There is perhaps no greater stress to a relationship than the addition of children. Kids are taxing physically, emotionally, and psychologically. They try patience and energy that should be going to your mate. But perhaps more than that, children provide a distraction that takes away from the hard work couples should be engaged in to fix their marriage. Since developmentally a child cannot see us in the kind of deep way we need to heal our loneliness, children can only exacerbate the feelings of solitude within a relationship.

According to Midrash, the birth of Cain and Abel does just this for Adam and Eve. Though Adam returns to Eve, their relationship is not healed. In fact, the same brokenness that existed before their sons' birth remains, so that years later when one day Cain rises up and kills Abel, Adam again flees from his wife. His relationship with her is not strong enough to survive the heartache of losing a child, and he fears that if he stays with her, he might have other children who could cause him pain. This time, Adam flees for 130 years (*Genesis Rabbah* 20:11). It will not be until Adam meets Adah and Zillah, two women who have fled from their husband Lamech after his killing of Cain and Tubal-cain, that he recognizes his hypocrisy (*Genesis Rabbah* 23:4). He counsels them to return, and he goes home to Eve.

Reconnection Is Possible

But this time, when Adam returns home, something miraculous happens. Our Rabbis teach that until this moment, Adam never desired his wife until he was in her presence. His desire was more animalistic than emotional. Like a dog who does not crave food until he smells it, Eve did not dwell in Adam's consciousness when he was not with her. She, by all accounts, did not exist for him until she stood beside him. Eve must have known this, which might have only exacerbated her feelings of loneliness. When Adam returns, however, he begins to desire her when she is with him and when she is not (*Genesis Rabbah* 23:5). Like a healthy relationship, she begins to occupy space in his thoughts and daydreams. Eve exists to Adam at all times now, and they begin steps to heal their relationship.

There is little question that Eve's marriage was not easy. But unlike many of the other examples in the Bible discussed in this book, Eve's story ends well. Midrash teaches that Eve was beside Adam when he died and was buried next to him in the cave of Machpelah (*Genesis Rabbah* 58:4). They would live out eternity conscious of each other and very much in love. While Eve acts as a kindred spirit to those who suffer loneliness in marital relationships, she also shows us one important truth: sometimes there is a return and a reconnection.

The Loneliness of Divorce

No one enters a marriage expecting to get divorced. We have high hopes on our wedding day. We envision the families we will start, the experiences we will share, and the dreams we will fulfill. But as the days pass, in the ebb tide of time, marriages fall apart.

Every instance of loneliness in this book is tragic, but divorce is the only personal calamity to which Judaism ascribes heavenly failure. Our tradition teaches that since the creation of the world, God has been busy making matches, and it's no easy task. To match a couple, says Rabbi Yosi, is as hard for God as splitting the Sea of Reeds (*Genesis Rabbah* 68:4). It's no surprise then that when we divorce, our pain is echoed in the cosmos. It is said that in ancient days, when two people would get divorced, even the altar in the Temple of Jerusalem would shed tears (Talmud, *Gittin* 90b).

Though there are other instances of divorce in our tradition, the story of Hagar and Abraham's divorce can teach us much about the particular loneliness that is present when a marriage dissolves.

The Humiliation of Being Cast Out

Hagar and Abraham find one another through a suggestion. Abraham's wife Sarah is old and unable to conceive a child. One day, Sarah presents her slave Hagar to Abraham, hoping that if she bears a child through him, it will become a proxy for the child that she cannot create. However, Sarah is not prepared for the results of this union. Hagar soon conceives, and Sarah finds herself filled with animosity. She punishes and abuses Hagar until finally Hagar runs away.

Finding herself alone in the desert, Hagar encounters an angel of God, who tells her that soon she will bear a child named Ishmael. God has heard her cries and is asking that she return home to Sarah. If she listens, she will be blessed.

Hagar does return home and time quickly passes. Ishmael grows up and Hagar grows older. Then Sarah bears a son, named Isaac. After his weaning, Sarah observes something unseemly between her son and Ishmael. The Rabbis abound with explanations,[7] but more important than the events of that day is their outcome. Sarah is angry and decides that Hagar and Ishmael must be banished. She approaches Abraham and demands that he send them off. At first, Abraham is distressed by this plea, but God intervenes, telling Abraham to listen to Sarah and promising that a great nation will emerge from Hagar and Ishmael. The next day Abraham throws Hagar and their son out.

On the surface, Hagar was like most other slaves. As chattel, she could come and go without the kind of emotional repercussions that weigh deeply on all of us when a household falls apart. Yet, despite the arguments to the contrary, our Rabbis saw Hagar and Abraham's relationship differently. The Bible is explicit about the nature of their union. Hagar was to be Abraham's wife (see Genesis 16:3). "A wife," the midrash reminds us, "not [just] as a concubine" (*Genesis Rabbah* 45:3). In being husband and wife, their parting would engender all the pain and messiness that dwells when marriages dissolve.

We can easily identify with Hagar on the day of her expulsion. There is a humiliation in the way she is cast out. That morning Abraham wakes up early, takes bread and a skin of water, and places it on Hagar's shoulders. Reflecting on this act, Israeli writer Meir Shalev writes, "Abraham set the pack on the shoulder, like putting something on a clothes hanger or in a saddlebag."[8] Then, our Rabbis tell us, he ties a water barrel to her loins so it would drag after her as she walked (*Pirke D'Rabbi Eliezer* 30). One can only imagine the scene of Hagar walking into the wilderness, holding her only provisions along with her child, a line in the sand growing more faint as she limps toward oblivion.

Wounded and Wandering

That moment in Hagar's life is the perfect metaphor for the loneliness inherent in divorce. When relationships end, many people engage in a sort of wandering. We've lived our lives moving in one direction only to find ourselves with a future open like a vast expanse. Many of my congregants have spoken to me about how overwhelming it feels to wake up rudderless, without a bearing.

I know this feeling well. Before my divorce, I knew where I wanted to go. I had a vision of my family one, two, five, ten, and thirty years down the line. I had experiences I was ready to share and goals I was ready to achieve. But as the truth sunk in that I was getting divorced, I suddenly realized I would need to rewrite those dreams. I remember sharing a beer with a friend and repeating, "I can't believe I have to start over again. I don't want to start over again." Attaining those dreams, having children and growing old with someone, seemed one step removed from reality. Yes, I would need to mourn my marriage and figure out what I was looking for in a future wife. But I would also need to rewrite and rediscover myself. I had lived so long attached to another, a piece of me belonged to her, and when I got divorced, I had to relinquish it. I couldn't find love again until I had filled in the part of me that I lost when my marriage ended with parts of myself that I could be proud of. If I had listed the fundamental nouns of my identity, "husband" would have been included in the top five alongside "rabbi," "son," "brother," and "Jew." For me, the thought of redefining myself was daunting. I was entering into the expanse of possibilities and was overwhelmed by its breadth. Like Hagar, I did not know where I would go, only that I must keep walking forward.

Though Hagar is carrying so much, she perhaps leaves more behind. More than even the physical things you lose when you split up a shared life, the people you lose can leave you feeling lonely and adrift. We all have three types of friendships. There are those that have a connection to us. There are others that are primarily connected though our spouse. Then, there are the friendships that are connected not to the people in a couple, but to the unit itself. When that unit breaks down, we almost always lose these last two categories, and the number of people who could become our potential confidants shrinks significantly. This was true for Hagar, who we must imagine formed deep friendships with the other slaves in Abraham's camp.

The Isolating Feeling of Failure

It's not just the directionless wanderings of Hagar that speaks to the experience of getting divorced but also her burden. Our tradition describes two reasons why Abraham tied the water jug around her waist, and both speak volumes to the nature of her suffering. In one opinion, the line in the sand caused by dragging the water alerted everyone to the fact that she was a handmaiden, cast out. Like the letter "A" that Hester Prynne wore in Hawthorne's *The Scarlet Letter*, the water jug and the mark it left as she walked would alert all who saw her of a shame in her past.

It's not shameful to get divorced. In fact, in many circumstances our tradition encourages it. Our Rabbis compare a bad relationship to living in a den with a snake (Talmud, *Yevamot* 112b) or dealing with a bad plague (*Yevamot* 63b). Some relationships are physically or emotionally abusive. In others, a member destroys the bonds of trust so deeply that the damage is irreconcilable. In still others, one or both members of the couple changes and the relationship cannot keep up with these transformations. Most of the time when one chooses to divorce, there is a good argument to be made for why this decision is right.

However, just because divorce is not shameful does not mean that it doesn't elicit feelings of shame. I remember in the months after my divorce feeling just like Hagar looked. I was weighed down by my burden. I was worried that when everyone looked at me, they would see failure. I feared that as I walked through life, I too would leave a mark in the sand behind me. This would be a sign to future relationships and potential friends that I was broken. I began rehearsing the "story" of why I got divorced, hoping that if I was able to explain the events well enough, I could somehow explain away the stigma I was expecting to see.

Our tradition does not help this feeling. In our Torah, the laws of divorce begin with a description of a man who marries a woman who eventually "fails to please him because he finds something obnoxious about her" (Deuteronomy 24:1). While our Rabbis argue about what would cause a woman to become obnoxious,[9] it's clear that the plain meaning of the text implies that if you are divorced, it must mean that there is something wrong with your character. Divorce informs us that we are stained, and our tradition agrees. For every statement in the Talmud that says that divorce is important and good, there is another that tells us that if a man divorces his wife he is to be detested.[10]

The Discomfort in What Remains

My story was different from many others. Because I got divorced so young, I was able to fully start again. My story and history were my only burden, and unlike Hagar, I was not carrying a person along as well. It is fitting that even though Ishmael was at an age when he could walk, he is described as being placed atop Hagar's shoulders when she left Abraham.[11] As she walked away, Hagar could feel the weight of her responsibility and feel the child that would tie her inextricably to her ex-husband.

As I mentioned above, the Rabbis imagined two reasons for why Hagar might need to drag the water jug behind her. If the first was to alert others of her shame, the second was to show Abraham her location. Our midrash explains that Abraham hoped that the line created by dragging her cargo would allow him to discover her new home, when ready and reunite with Ishmael. He would remain involved in his son's life because despite the distance, her footprints would point the way.

Eventually, Abraham would go to visit his son. The Rabbis imagine two such visits. However, before each journey, Sarah would implore her husband, "Go, but don't get off your camel." Abraham acceded and journeyed to Ishmael with the mandate to keep his distance. Leaving aside the obvious anguish this might have caused his son, we can also imagine the deep isolation this act engendered in Hagar. He would visit but would not stand on the same soil as her.

I've talked to many congregants who, because of children, still interact with their former spouses. For some this relationship can morph into a deep friendship, but for others the natural boundaries that form, boundaries we set up with most people in our lives, seem alien and puritanical when they mediate between two people who once shared so much. If, as we will see, part of the response to loneliness is finding those rare people who can truly see you, it is devastating when you lose one of them. But the cruelty of divorce is that in its aftermath, we are often in proximity of that person without access to their intimacy. They remain "on the camel," at arm's length but close enough to remind us what we lost.

Yet, even without a child, we can't fully break the tie to our former lovers. There is a teaching in our tradition that, while problematic, contains a degree of truth:

> "Do not cook in a pot where your neighbor has cooked."
> What does that mean? Do not marry a divorced
> woman while her husband is still living. For a master

said: When a divorced man marries a divorced woman,
there are four yearnings in bed. (Talmud, *Pesachim* 112a)

Leaving aside the example the Rabbis use—though some people do
think of their former lovers while intimate with their current ones—
we may find that our former spouses occupy our thoughts at inopportune times. We can distance ourselves from another, and we can purge
our houses of joint possessions, but we cannot control when they will
appear in our memories. We may move on; we may have wonderful
first dates and amazing moments of love. We may share engagements,
weddings, and children with another. Yet, at these important transitional moments, it's not unnatural to be reminded that you have done
this before. Ironically, few people can share this with their new spouse.
Bringing up the past may feel like we are taking away from the present.
Instead, we keep it bottled up, and that only adds to the alienation of
divorce and reinforces the perception that others do not understand.

Even if others overlook the nuances of our loneliness, our tradition does not. Hagar is emblematic of the complexities of divorce. Like
any trauma, it is helpful to have affirmation that what we are feeling is
acceptable and that someone understands. Hagar, whose name means
"stranger," becomes our intimate confidant. There are few people who
can accept the true ambivalence that comes when a relationship ends—
how we can be relieved and saddened, open and guarded, devastated
and hopeful. Hagar is a model for all those suffering, a quiet voice from
afar who whispers, "It's okay, I've been there too."

3

The Loneliness
of Leadership

How Responsibility Can Drive Us Apart

The Pain of Telling Hard Truths

Judaism's born truth tellers are the prophets. They live lives of integrity, standing up for their ideals even in the face of opposition. Chosen by God, their sole task is to convey God's word to the people. Sometimes this word will be comforting and pleasant, but often it is harsh and unyielding. Abraham Joshua Heschel summarized the plight of the prophet best:

> The prophet is a lonely man. He alienates the wicked as well as the pious, the cynics as well as the believers, the priests and the princes, the judges and the false prophets. But to be a prophet means to challenge and to defy and to cast out fear.[1]

Perhaps no prophet feels the pain of alienation and the ostracism of communicating God's word more than the prophet Jeremiah. Jeremiah had a way of conveying God's anger that few others in history can touch. In fact, his warnings to ancient Israel were considered so stern that a specific rhetorical style was named for him: a jeremiad is literary rebuke of society that reveals the anger and the disgust of the speaker.

Our Rabbis tell us that even from a young age Jeremiah knew he would be the recipient of the people's ire. The Rabbis imagine that when God called him to the task of prophecy, Jeremiah spoke up: "Master of the universe, I cannot prophesy to them. What prophet ever came before them who they did not seek to slay?" Jeremiah had learned that the lives of previous prophets were dark. Moses, Elijah, Elisha— all spoke God's words and were condemned for it (*Pirke D'Rabbi Eliezer* 26:1–2). Jeremiah is not the first prophet to resist God's call. When asked to confront Pharaoh and request that he free the Israelites from slavery, Moses famously replied to God, "I am slow of speech and slow of tongue" (Exodus 4:10). However, Jeremiah's reluctance is unique. While other prophets resisted God's call because they worried that they were not up to the task, Jeremiah knew he had the skill to speak God's message to the people. His was a much more visceral response. He knew that stepping into the role of prophet would distance himself from his family and community.

Trading Community for Role

Jeremiah was correct; his life would be one of distance. Early on in his career, Jeremiah receives a message from God, "You are not to marry and not to have sons or daughters in this place" (Jeremiah 16:1). Though the message is opaque, Jeremiah soon learns why. Although he, as God's messenger, is immune from God's wrath, his family will not be. God tells him, "They shall die gruesome deaths. They shall not be lamented or buried; they shall be like dung on the surface of the ground" (Jeremiah 16:4). Jeremiah can have children if he wants, but because he is privy to the future suffering of his family, he will spend his whole life worrying about when the ax will fall. Sadly, the price he pays to avoid the pain of losing his children and wife will be a life without their support and love. He never marries. His loneliness is the cost of saving them from suffering.

While plenty of people live fulfilling lives without family, communities that serve as powerful substitutes usually surround them. However, these too are unavailable to Jeremiah. Because of his role as prophet, Jeremiah lacks connection with his community. He cannot cultivate friendships and does not connect with peers. The reason for his solitude is twofold. Directly, God commands Jeremiah to avoid relationships with his neighbors. In order to effectively do his job as God's mouthpiece, Jeremiah is warned to avoid events of communal cohesion, like weddings or funerals. God tells him:

> Do not enter a house of mourning; do not go to lament
> and to condole with them; for I have withdrawn My
> favor from that people.... Nor shall you enter a house
> of feasting, to sit down with them to eat and drink....
> I am going to banish from this place, in your days and
> before your eyes, the sound of mirth and gladness, the
> voice of bridegroom and bride. (Jeremiah 16:5, 16:8–9)

As a prophet, Jeremiah is an emissary of God. His task is to create a microcosm of heaven for the people. As a stand-in for the Divine, how can he accurately convey the distance between God and Israel if he becomes too intimate with his peers? Showing up for their highest and lowest moments would send the message that God has forgiven them. Moreover, by telling him to keep his distance, God is telling Jeremiah not to waste his time with the people. It is as if God is saying, "They may be dancing now, but soon they will be mourning. They may need comfort now, but they have no idea the comfort they will need soon."

Anyone who has ever danced with a bride and groom on their wedding day or gazed wholeheartedly into the eyes of a mourner knows that these touchstones are truly platforms for genuine connection. Throughout his life Jeremiah is commanded to speak *at* the people, not *with* them. He is encouraged to be among the people, but not of them. Though our Rabbis tell us that Jeremiah, more than perhaps any other prophet, would find himself in close proximity to the people—he would often prophesy in city squares rather than in the Temple or in the home—his physical closeness to the people would not bring connection (*Pesikta Rabbati* 26:1/2). As we have established, connection is not formed in crowds. It is formed in the home around the dinner table, at synagogue during prayer, in the study hall, and at the peaks and valleys of human experience. Loneliness is healed through intentional moments of connection. And Jeremiah is denied all of these.

Disdain Leads to Loneliness

We can only imagine that as painful as it was to miss moments of connection in society, Jeremiah might have been able to tolerate his solitude if he were liked. Sadly, throughout the Bible, Jeremiah meets scorn at nearly every turn. As a prophet, Jeremiah is set up to be the bad guy. Watching him spit vitriol over their lives, his community cannot separate his task of speaking God's truth from his person. His inconvenient message makes him an inconvenience. In perhaps the most heartbreaking passage in his book, Jeremiah speaks about the isolation of prophecy:

> I have become a constant laughingstock. Everyone jeers at me. For every time I speak, I must cry out, must shout, "Lawlessness and rapine!" For the word of God causes me constant disgrace and contempt. I thought, "I will not mention Him. No more will I speak His name"— but [His word] was like a raging fire in my heart, shut up in my bones; I could not hold it in, I was helpless. I heard the whispers of the crowd—terror all around: "Inform! Let us inform against him!" All my [supposed] friends are waiting for me to stumble: "Perhaps he can be entrapped, and we can prevail against him and take our vengeance on him." (Jeremiah 20:7–10)

The tragedy of this statement is evident. Jeremiah is constantly taunted for doing God's will. He speaks but the people will not believe him. They are waiting for him to err. For if he does, he will be seen as a false prophet and will be punished for corrupting God's word. It is painful to be believed and hated for your message, but Jeremiah has it much worse. He is not believed and hated nonetheless. Like Cassandra of Greek lore, who was driven mad by the curse of speaking true prophecies that no one would heed, Jeremiah would face the consistent alienation of speaking truth to deaf ears.

Speaking Truth to Deaf Ears

Although we are not prophets like Jeremiah, many of us have faced the loneliness of delivering a message that was not received. I've always been struck by the image of Martin Luther King, a prophet himself, who like his biblical ancestor was thrown in prison for his perceived iconoclasm—Jeremiah for defying the Benjaminites,[2] King after a series of marches and sit-ins. While behind bars in the Birmingham jail, King wrote of the loneliness of being a prophet. Citing the "real heroes" of the South, he praised the "Negro sit-inners and demonstrators of Birmingham for their sublime courage, their willingness to suffer, and their amazing discipline in the midst of great provocation."[3] King then turned to the character of James Meredith, who lived "with the noble sense of purpose that enables them to face jeering and hostile mobs, and with the agonizing loneliness that characterizes the life of the pioneer."[4] For King and Meredith, their purpose led them to face malice and hate. Like Jeremiah, and like all prophets today who speak the truth to hostile ears, their pursuit of good made them pariahs.

Even if we aren't advocating for grand purposes like racial equality, we can feel like scorned prophets. We all have truths we wish to convey and messages we hope to share. Like the prophet who seeks out a response to his plea, we seek out responses to ours. We ask friends to change behaviors, family members to be more present in our lives, bosses to be more open. But, like Jeremiah, we are sometimes silenced, even despised for our revelation. Our message falls on deaf ears. It is a lonely experience to share a message of intimacy and hope and to know it was ignored. Jeremiah symbolizes for us every offering for connection that was not returned.

When Failure Leads to Blame

Left without a community, Jeremiah must turn to the one source that he knows might listen. Throughout the Bible, Jeremiah seeks a connection with God, who placed him in his solitary position in the first place. As time goes on, however, the wedge between the two grows ever wider. God becomes little help for Jeremiah. In fact, God blames Jeremiah for his predicament. Toward the middle of the book, God tells Jeremiah he has failed because he is weak. "If you race with the foot-runners and they exhaust you," God says, "how then can you compete with horses? If you are secure only in a tranquil land, how will you fare in the jungle of the Jordan?" (Jeremiah 12:5). By reminding Jeremiah that he, not his people, is incapable, God alienates Jeremiah from his task and destroys his self-worth. God's rebuke forces Jeremiah to internalize his own inadequacies, pulling him even further from society. In one particular telling episode in his life, Jeremiah cries out in self-pity to his mother, who "bore me, a man of conflict and strife with all the land!" (Jeremiah 15:10).

The increasing distance with God forces Jeremiah into anger. Instead of taking steps to get back into God's graces, Jeremiah rebukes God: "You enticed me, O God, and I was enticed; You overpowered me and You prevailed" (Jeremiah 20:7). In another outburst, Jeremiah blames God directly for his loneliness, telling God that his prophetic task has forced him apart from the community and kept him from sharing their joy: "I have sat lonely because of Your hand upon me; for You have filled me with gloom" (Jeremiah 15:17).

Finding Value in Purpose

Jeremiah's distance from God is tragic because without God, he is utterly alone. When he lost his connection to God, Jeremiah lost something much more important—the reinforcement that his mission had value. A person needs two things to find fulfillment: purpose and relationship. Sometimes, however, we can sacrifice one for the other. We can allow ourselves to be isolated as long as we feel that good will come from it. Reading Jeremiah's story, we can only imagine that when he realized the futility of his task, when he saw that his words were in vain and that they served only to distance him from God, he realized his pain had been for naught.

If only Jeremiah knew that despite his suffering, his prophecy would find life in future days. If only he knew that though he lacked a family in his time, he would find a place among the generations in ours. If only he learned that his message would one day not be met with deafness but would inspire countless to seek righteousness. Jeremiah teaches the prophets among us, those dreamers whose message is inconvenient and whose passions are just, that though we might face failure today, history can redeem our loneliness and our words can find a coveted place at the feet of those to come.

The Loneliness of Political Leadership

Throughout his life, King David faced much suffering. He lost his best friend Jonathan on the battlefield, his children assaulted and killed one another, and one of his sons, Absalom, rebelled against him, forcing him to flee Jerusalem. Yet, David was lonely apart from these events. For him, the very act of being the king was enough to bring about suffering and isolation. The death, sickness, and rebellion he faced in life were beside the point.

David's greatest error, the seduction of Bathsheba, gives us a profound window into his loneliness. Many of us know the story (2 Samuel 11). One day David sees a beautiful woman bathing on the roof of a nearby building. Bringing her into this court, he sleeps with her and impregnates her. There is one problem: Bathsheba is already married to a man named Uriah the Hittite. David calls Uriah back from the battlefront, hoping he will sleep with his wife so that David's child will be confused for his. Uriah refuses to go home, however, reminding David that he can't enjoy time with his wife when his comrades are dying on the battlefield. Knowing he will be discovered, David decides to send Uriah to the very front line of the battle, where he will be killed, thus erasing the only person who might question his son's paternity. Soon the child is born, and God punishes David; because of David's misdeeds, the child will die in infancy. He will not see him grow up.

The story of David and Bathsheba is painful at nearly every turn. While there is often something comforting about one of our greatest ancestors having flaws, the flaws that shine through in this story seem too acute. David is tyrannical and opportunistic. He abuses his power and is callous. Yet, in the rush to get to this tale of scandal and intrigue, we often gloss over the first few lines, which paint David as incredibly isolated and lonely. Though they cannot excuse his actions, they certainly can let us peek into David's psyche and teach us about the alienation of holding power.

Lacking Companionship at the Top

The narrative of David and Bathsheba begins with an introduction that describes the timing of the scene. It is the season when kings go out to battle, yet David, for some unknown reason, is confined to his palace. Left alone, and apart from the men he commands, David awakens toward evening, wallowing the day away, apart from everyone who knows him (2 Samuel 11:1–2). In fact, the Malbim, one of the nineteenth century's most famous biblical commentators, reminds us that David would often eat alone during those times, and with little to do but gorge himself, he would slip into a sort of food coma and awake late. Arising from his bed, David makes his way out to the roof of his house. He is alone, walking pensively. He looks out and sees Bathsheba bathing. But David is companionless. No one is around him when he first views her, and the Bible tells us that he must send for others and wait so he can ask who this mysterious woman is. Learning her identity, he sends for her.

Our Rabbis understood David's profound loneliness in this moment. While a king is always surrounded by people, it doesn't mean these are meaningful relationships. Likewise, while David had other wives, it didn't mean these relationships could sustain him. In a somewhat audacious midrash, the Rabbis see the line "Late one afternoon, David rose from his couch" (2 Samuel 11:2) to mean that he had just had marital relations with another of his wives (Talmud, *Sanhedrin* 107a). Like Eve in our previous chapter, David's carnal relations are unsatisfying. David has a hunger. In the Rabbinic imagination, this hunger is a sexual yearning that served as a symptom of an insatiable appetite for connection that he could not achieve even in the bedroom, the most intimate of realms.

David's pain is familiar to many who have served in positions of leadership. It's lonely at the top. A king has to carry the fate of his people on his shoulders, but as the final arbiter, no one is there to carry your fate. Leadership is structured like a reverse pyramid; the more power you have, the fewer the numbers who can support you when you fall and the less hands there are to share responsibility with you. For this reason, we know of countless politicians, entrepreneurs, and business executives who have faced isolation and solitude as part of their professional lives. In fact, a 2012 study found that 50 percent of all CEOs experience significant loneliness as part of their professional life, with 70 percent of first-time CEOs claiming that their loneliness adversely affects their job performance.[5]

One reason for this is because, as a public figure, everyone knows a piece of you, but few know the whole you. Intimacy begets understanding, but too often leaders do not have the opportunity to let others in. I know our president by his role. I know how he speaks at the podium, but not how he speaks to his children. I've seen him cry for our country, but not for a loved one at a funeral. Public figures occupy two spaces; we know parts of their life deeply, while other parts of their life are invisible to us. But because we cannot allow people to remain only partially familiar to us, we fill in the gaps of what we don't know with what we want them to be. Public figures are the only people we have permission to deeply love or hate without actually knowing enough about them to make the decision. This is exacerbated by a phenomenon present in the lives of political leaders like David: because their decisions directly affect our lives for better or worse, their policy positions become referenda on their character. They are bad people if they make our lives worse, even if it makes our country better.

Ironically, public figures have a surprisingly little amount of power when it comes to their public image. How lonely it is to look out at a rally or concert and know that people are judging your character based on your persona. To make matters worse, they are using judgments of you as social capital. Speaking about this phenomenon in regard to celebrities like Britney Spears, cultural critic Chuck Klosterman writes:

> Every day, random people use Britney's existence as currency; they talk about her public failures and her lack of talent as a way to fill the emptiness of their own normalcy.... [And because of this] she doesn't earn a fraction of what she warrants in a free-trade cultural

economy. If Britney Spears were paid $1 every time a self-loathing stranger used her as a surrogate for his own failure, she would outearn Warren Buffet in three months.[6]

Power Mutes Our True Selves

Additionally, leaders are not always given the leeway to be fully vulnerable. As we will see toward the end of this book, vulnerability is the avenue to connection. Yet, one's office too often takes precedence over one's person. Does the CEO have the freedom to look weak at his board meeting? Can a politician voice ambivalence over her own policy positions? There is a teaching in the Talmud that speaks directly to this experience. Observing that many positions of power deserve respect, our Rabbis ask the question, can an elder, teacher, or king all renounce the honor due to them, allowing another to sit in their presence while they stand or permitting someone to contradict them when speaking? (*Kiddushin* 32a–b). Though a strong case is made for why elders or teachers might be permitted to renounce their honor, all agree that it is inappropriate for a king to do so. The Rabbis explain the reason for this ruling simply: a king can do his job only if the awe of the people is upon him. In other words, if a king is too close to the people he leads, he will not have the power to command. At times of war or crisis, people need to be moved to action, and distance ensures the power to do this.

King David's loneliness results from his inability to be fully himself. In fact, when he tries to show it to the people, he is rebuked. One of the most genuine moments in David's life is when he brings the Holy Ark into Jerusalem to consecrate his newly ordained capital. Ecstatic and excited, David dances "with all his might" (2 Samuel 6:14). The Bible is uncharacteristically descriptive of David's movements. He is leaping and spinning, caught up in the moment. David is so overjoyed by the events of the day that he fails to notice that his skirt is riding up. When he returns home, he meets the ire of his wife Michal: "Didn't the king of Israel do himself honor today—exposing himself today in the sight of the slavegirls of his subjects, as one of the riffraff might expose himself!"

(2 Samuel 6:20). David responds to Michal with unimagined cruelty, reminding her of her dead father's flaws and condemning her to a life of isolation, in part from the realization that she is correct. In that moment he realizes that he can never fully be part of the people. From that point on, David never again dances before God. His passion is tempered by his prestige.

The Alienation of the Creative Soul

There is one more thing that isolates leaders like King David. The great leaders of a generation must be many things; some are strong, others thoughtful, many dynamic, but nearly all must have a degree of creativity. Our tradition tells us that David, a musician and poet, was brimming with genius. It was what allowed him to choose the rock over the sword in his battle with Goliath, write the psalms, and play the harp that soothed King Saul's soul. Yet, rather than draw him closer to others, that creativity served as a roadblock. David was so caught up in the sublime and transcendent embodied in his genius that he was unable to connect to the everyday world. We all know leaders like this, those who value ideas over people, imagination over connection. In fact, as Philip Roth argues, sometimes to be a great creator one must eschew meaningful relationships to focus on his or her work in solitude.[7]

This might have been why David stayed behind when his people went to war. Our tradition tells us that David did not sleep at night. Lying in bed, his mind was racing. He was distracted by everything, even the sound of the wind tickling the strings of his harp. Eventually, our tradition teaches, David would arise, light a candle, and continue writing (Talmud, *Berachot* 4a). A king cannot command when he cannot sleep. David spent the night in the isolation of insomnia. When the world was asleep, he was imprisoned by wakefulness, and during the day he was crippled by exhaustion.

However, all of King David's lonely experiences, his isolation as a leader, his distance from the people, his creativity, even his insomnia made David into the wellspring of insight and depth of character we know today. If, as the tradition states, David wrote the book of Psalms, then David's solitude gave us many of the most profound lines of isolation anywhere in the Western canon. David's loneliness was the catalyst that allowed his broken spirit to come alive through the written word. He is one of the most colorful characters in the Bible because of his rich reservoir of pain.

David wrote with a hand of profound pathos and wisdom. "Look at my right and see," he wrote, "I have no friend; there is nowhere I can flee, no one cares about me" (Psalm 142:5). "Turn to me, have mercy on me, for I am alone and afflicted" (Psalm 25:16). David was a lonely leader in his time, but is a voice of comfort in ours. His people may not have understood him, but we certainly do. His work is his window. He reaches out through it across the generations.

The Loneliness of Religious Leadership

Much of what made David lonely can be seen in the character of Aaron, Moses's brother and the first High Priest of ancient Israel. Unlike David, however, Aaron wasn't simply a political leader. Though he certainly shared political functions, he was foremost a religious leader, and this distinction comes with a host of other challenges that even a king does not face.

Perhaps one of the loneliest episodes of Aaron's life appears in the moments before the building of the golden calf. According to the Bible, the people become afraid when Moses climbs Sinai to receive the Torah from God and is delayed in returning. They approach Aaron and ask him to build them a physical representation of God. Aaron asks the people to take off their gold jewelry. He melts down the gold and casts it into a mold, forming the image. The next day, he proclaims a festival to God, making the calf the centerpiece of the celebration (Exodus 32:1–8).

Perplexed as to why such a righteous person would facilitate this celebration and promote idolatry, our Rabbis looked outside the story for an explanation. They noticed that a central character and one of Moses's key advisors in the book of Exodus, named Hur, disappeared from the Bible after the golden calf incident. With this key piece of information, they developed a creative explanation. According to Midrash, the people originally come to Hur to ask him to build them an idol. He rejects their plea, and in an angry outburst they kill him. They then turn to Aaron with the same request. Seeing Hur lying dead below him, Aaron knows he has no choice. It is better that he build an idol for which the people might eventually find forgiveness than deny their request and risk a second murder (Talmud, *Sanhedrin* 7a).

We can only imagine Aaron's isolation at the moment of Hur's death. Hur, though not prevalent in the preceding narrative, was prominent. Hur stood beside Moses and Aaron as the Israelites fought against the Amalekites and he physically held Moses's hands up as inspiration during the battle (Exodus 17:12). Hur was also part of the entourage who went up to Sinai with Moses and was tasked with dealing with legal matters in his stead (Exodus 24:12–14). In a way, Hur stood on equal ground with Aaron. If the people were willing to kill him for not listening, then Aaron was not immune.

Aaron knew this as he watched the people murder Hur. But he also knew something else that was incredibly tragic: Hur died wearing a mask. Despite his character, the people saw him only for his role. They needed him to facilitate their religious experience, and if he could not do this, then he was of no use. It didn't matter that he had a family—his grandson Bezalel would go on to be the architect of the Tabernacle— only that he be willing to say yes.

Projection and the Loss of Self

Aaron's loneliness is unique in the Bible, and it is present today in the lives of religious leaders. Today, there are many people who may be considered prophets but few who might be called priests. Whereas a prophet takes a truth and conveys it to the people, the priest takes the prayers and yearnings of the people and conveys them to God. Like Aaron, he or she is the avenue through which the people attain divine connection. Yet, anytime a person's main role is as a conduit, it is easy to confuse their person for their task, and as we have observed, losing your sense of self is one of the chief causes of loneliness.

Once in rabbinical school, I had the task of leading a school-wide service. As part of the recitation of the *Kaddish*, the Jewish memorial prayer, I was tasked with reading the names of the donors and teachers who had died during that week throughout the years. That particular day happened to be the *yahrzeit* (memorial anniversary) of the founder of the school, Isaac Mayer Wise. I paused when I reached his name and acknowledged him, but I did not separate his name out from the list.

Later, at a school-wide debrief of services, an elderly professor stood up and berated me publicly for disgracing Wise's memory. How could I keep a man like this together with all these less significant names? It took me a while to realize that in the moment of reading these names, I wasn't me. I was instead a representative of memory in the Jewish community. This professor was worried that he would not be honored after his own death. If we didn't raise up the memory of Isaac Mayer Wise, then surely his name would end up buried in the list soon after he was gone. At that moment, it didn't matter that I was just a student. It didn't matter that I had tried my best. The task of commemoration, the burden of memorial, was on me. Because the stakes are so high, errors have added meaning for religious leaders.

Furthermore, since the task of a religious leader involves helping others connect with God, we sometimes are mistaken for God altogether. One of the loneliest experiences I ever had as a rabbi occurred while officiating at a wedding during a hurricane. Arriving early, I began to set up my materials. I noticed that the room that we had intended for signing the *ketubah* (marriage contract) lacked a table. I approached the mother of the groom and asked where I might find a table. Immediately, her demeanor changed. She began yelling at me, telling me that two-thirds of her guests had canceled that day and that I needed to be patient. Then, as quickly as she exploded, she grew calm and helped me find the table.

There was injustice in the way I was attacked. Yes, I could have led with an acknowledgment that the day might be difficult, but I was polite in my request and pleasant in my demeanor. I knew this woman and had always had friendly interactions with her. It took me a while to realize that in that moment, she was not yelling at me. Rather, she was angry with God for the hurricane that ruined her son's wedding. For her, the storm was one of the greatest injustices of her life. She couldn't scream at God, but she could berate *me*. That day, I served the necessary role of divine proxy.

What made these stories so alienating was that in both cases, I had no control over how I would be seen. Like Aaron, my role as religious leader negated my individuality and identity. If either person had truly seen me, they would not have attacked with such force. Instead, they saw what I stood for, and this was a worthy target. It's hard to feel close to others when you can't trust them to separate you from your purpose.

Our tradition understands how easy it is to privilege role over person. There is little doubt that Aaron was considered one of the most spiritual, compassionate, and devoted religious leaders of all time. Yet, say our Rabbis, if Aaron had lived at a later generation under the religious leadership of someone less gifted than him, he would still hold less authority than the person with a higher title (*Ecclesiastes Rabbah* 1:4). It doesn't matter how loving or connected Aaron was. People see the role above the person, and without that role he was nothing.

All of this must have gone through Aaron's mind at the moment he decided to help the people build the calf. His job was to facilitate divine connection, and the people were ready to destroy him if he forgot this. Aaron's story is powerful because of how deeply it warns us to be mindful of confusing a person with his or her title. If we are to alleviate the loneliness of those around us, then we shouldn't forget the inherent loneliness of being a religious caretaker.

4

The Loneliness of Sickness and Loss

Struggles Across the Life Cycle

The Loneliness of Mourning

Though there are many deaths in the Bible, we have only a few examples of actual mourners and even fewer examples of the pain that comes after losing a loved one. Characters as diverse as David, Abraham, and Jacob all mourn after a loss, but there is something unique about the loneliness that Isaac faces after the death of his mother, Sarah, that has always spoken to me.

We know little about Sarah's death. Our Torah tells us that she died at the age of 127 in Kiryat Arba, modern-day Hebron (Genesis 23:1). And, though we learn later of Isaac's pain, the spotlight following her passing is on her husband, Abraham. Abraham cries for her, eulogizes her, and seeks out a plot in which to bury her. Isaac is absent from the story. All we know is that following her burial, Abraham becomes concerned that his son will marry a Canaanite woman and sends his servant Eliezer to find him a wife from his father's birthplace.

It is only after the account of Eliezer traveling north, meeting Rebekah and her family, and convincing Rebekah to return home with him to marry his master's son that we first see Isaac. Our first glimpse of Isaac is not of a confident or excited patriarch. It is one of a suffering, pensive mourner. The Hebrew is difficult to translate. In Hebrew we are told that in the moments before meeting his wife, Isaac was *suach basadeh*, which has been translated as meditating, praying, or even wandering aimlessly through the field (Genesis 24:63). Whatever the meaning, there is a clear valence of pain in Isaac's action. A glance at the word's appearance in other parts of the Bible makes this clear. Psalm 102:1 reads, "A prayer of the lowly man when he is faint and pours forth his plea [*sicho*] before God," while Psalm 55:18 says, "Evening, and morning, and at noon, I will complain [*asichah*] and moan."

The Irreparable Pain of Loss

According to Midrash, Isaac has been lamenting for a long time; it has been three years since his mother died, and Isaac is still wandering the fields, lost and alone (*Pirke D'Rabbi Eliezer* 31). Although three years seems like an eternity to mourn, it's not uncommon to still feel broken many years after a loss. Losing someone you love is a process of taking steps forward and backward. One of the hardest parts of healing is the uncertainty that surrounds it. You never know when the rush of pain will hit you. I remember talking to one mourner who confessed that a decade after losing his mother he broke down in a supermarket because he saw an item of food that reminded him of his childhood meals. It is said that one explanation for why we tear our clothes after losing someone we love is because even if we mend that garment, it will never be the same; we will always have the remnant of the tear in it. Likewise, time may seek to repair our hearts following a loss, but its tear will always remain irreparable. As one congregant wisely told me when explaining the challenge of losing a parent, "You never get over the pain. You just get used to it."

The Other Things You Lose with Death

Although every mourner has a unique pain, the Rabbinic understanding of Isaac's pain is familiar and common to many. The Rabbis teach that after losing Sarah, four constants in Isaac's life disappeared:

> As long as Sarah lived a cloud hung over her tent [signifying God's presence]; when she died, that cloud

disappeared.... As long as Sarah lived, her doors were
wide open; at her death that liberality ceased.... As
long as Sarah lived, there was a blessing on her dough,
and the lamp used to burn from the evening of the Sabbath until the evening of the following Sabbath; when
she died these ceased. (*Genesis Rabbah* 60:16)

Each of these four constants symbolizes a different aspect of Isaac's life,
dimmed through the pain of losing his mother. For him, his mother
was a connection to God. Her religious spirit brought God close, and
when she passed away, Isaac felt himself far not only from her, but
also from his creator. He did not know how to access God without
her near. Sarah was also a connection to hospitality and openness. His
mother, who only a few chapters earlier brought food and drink to
three wandering men who stopped at her tent (Genesis 18:6), could
no longer open her doors for others. When she died, Isaac saw that the
world was a little less just. Then there was the loss of her piety. Dough
and lamps are meant to symbolize ritual connection. Sarah observed
the rituals of Shabbat as no other did and no other could. For Isaac, the
Sabbath would be less rich and beautiful without her in it.

Isaac's struggles as a mourner are expressed elsewhere by our ancient
Rabbis. Reflecting on what we really lose when a loved one passes away,
our tradition notes the gifts that were lost when certain sages died:

When Meir died, parables came to an end.
When Ben Azai died, scholarship disappeared.
When Akiva died, the glory of Torah dissolved.
When Chanina ben Dosa died, there were no more miracles.
(*MISHNAH SOTAH* 9:15)

Each of these rabbis stood for something more than themselves. They
embodied virtues like scholarship and wisdom, piety and pedagogy,
and when they were no more, it felt as if the world had lost their defining features as well. Similarly, Sarah's connection to God, her piety, her
sense of justice, and her ritual observance were so all-encompassing in
her life that they came to an end for Isaac. He was alienated from all

those things that he had loved alongside her, because he had no one to share them with.

There are so many today who suffer like Isaac after the death of a loved one. Isaac is the woman in my congregation who stopped eating chicken soup because the dish reminded her of her late husband. He is the parent who avoids entering the park where his son used to play soccer. He is the local rabbi who no longer prays personal prayers because of the distance he feels from God after his mother's passing.

Eventually, Isaac meets Rebekah and is able to find comfort. After years of pain "Isaac ... brought her into the tent of his mother Sarah, and he took Rebekah as his wife. Isaac loved her, and thus found comfort after his mother's death" (Genesis 24:67). Our Rabbis tell us that Rebekah had many of the same attributes Isaac missed in his mother. She brought God, justice, and ritual back to his life (*Genesis Rabbah* 60:16). For many, however, there is no easy fix. Not everyone wallowing in the field will have occasion to look up and see Rebekah from afar. Instead, we are left wandering alone, reflecting on the richness of the life that disappeared the day we lost that central figure in our lives. But though we may feel alone, we are not. Isaac is walking beside us, a companion in our pain. His story may not help us feel less lonely in our grief, but his presence in our tradition means we are not alone.

The Loneliness of Pregnancy Loss and Infertility

One of the most profound images in *Moby Dick* comes at the end of the novel. After the sinking of his ship, the *Pequod*, and adrift at sea, Ishmael floats through the water for a full day, grabbing hold of a coffin to keep from drowning. Eventually, he spots a ship named *Rachel* in the distance. The ship has been wandering, looking for a vessel that disappeared earlier while on a hunt for the great white whale. As the ship draws closer, the book ends with an observation: "It was the devious-cruising Rachel, that in her retracing search after her missing children, only found another orphan."[1]

It's no coincidence that the wandering ship, perhaps the loneliest character in the novel, was given the name *Rachel*. Throughout her life, the biblical Rachel suffered immensely. Though she would remain the favorite wife of her husband Jacob, the shame and alienation of infertility would haunt her throughout her days. The challenge of bearing children would leave her adrift and wandering, always yearning and searching for the missing children she wished she could hold. As the boat did for Ishmael, Rachel would adopt and care for the children of others. She would help raise her sister Leah's children and foster her concubines' sons as her own. Yet despite all of this, Rachel was still alone in her struggle to have children. Even with the births of her sons Joseph and Benjamin, Rachel would remain one of the central models of the loneliness a woman feels when she hopes for a family that she is unable to bear.

Infertility and Blame

Our tradition has much to say about the struggles of infertility. However, the problem with many of our most famous teachings about infertility is that they blame the victim. The Torah warns us that if we obey God, "none of your women and men will be childless" (Deuteronomy 7:14). Childbearing is so central to our tradition that our Midrash says, "He who has no son, it is as though he were dead, utterly demolished" (*Genesis Rabbah* 45:2). These statements castigate those who suffer and make it harder to seek support from a tradition that opens its arms to so many.

Yet, through stories like Rachel's, those who are struggling with infertility can find a kindred spirit and true reflection of pain. Like many who face struggles with pregnancy, Rachel faced blame at home. The failure of her womb became her failure. Our Rabbis warn us that God gives extra support to those dealing with infertility because of how easy it is to lose esteem in the eyes of others (*Genesis Rabbah* 71:2). Both the Torah and later midrashim contain accounts of incredibly hurtful statements made by Jacob to his wife. During one argument, captured in the Bible, Jacob assigns divine mandate to Rachel's barrenness: "Can I take the place of God, who has denied you fruit of the womb?" (Genesis 30:2). In another imagined conversation, the Rabbis explain that during this fight, Jacob blames Rachel for her fertility issues: "I have sons from Leah, so it couldn't be me who is defective" (*Genesis Rabbah* 71:7). Hearing this attack, Rachel does not remain silent. She criticizes her husband for failing to live up to the ideals set forth by his forebearers. She reminds Jacob that his father Isaac and grandfather Abraham both prayed to God when their wives were struggling with becoming pregnant. "Why," she seems to say, "would you blame me, rather than support and advocate for me?" Because of Jacob's callousness in the face of his wife's struggles, our Rabbis teach that it was decreed then that Rachel's son Joseph would one day stand in judgment before the rest of his children. Here, Rachel becomes a source of strength for later generations who refuse to be condemned for struggles outside of their control.

Rachel's story is not unique. Perhaps more than any other struggle outlined in this book, infertility includes the most blame. Because it's such a personal thing, many people are uncomfortable talking about it. Both women and men feel that they should naturally be able to have children, and they feel that whatever is going wrong in their bodies reflects poorly on them as people. There is so much shame around infertility, and when combined with the secrecy that often surrounds it, it is one of the loneliest and most destructive experiences a person or a couple can go through.

Infertility Rewrites Our Dreams

In addition to the shame and secrecy that surround it, infertility is devastating because of what it does to our personal stories. According to Janet Jaffe, author of the book *Unsung Lullabies*, when we decide to have children, we create a story in our head.[2] My daughter will play the trumpet and go to Harvard. My son will enroll in soccer and will one day take over the family business. We hope our children will have our eyes, her smile, his laugh, and we live out our child's future in our dreams. Each month couples wait anxiously to find out whether they have succeeded in starting a family, and each month they are reminded with a physical sign that they were not successful. For them, menstruation or a miscarriage signals not just a loss but a death of this manifestation of their dream.

The Feeling of Banishment

Classically, *niddah* is the term used for a woman who is menstruating and becomes ritually impure through her blood. Though today many struggle with the connotation that there is anything wrong with a woman who has her period, the original meaning of the term is apt for those struggling with infertility. *Niddah* comes from the Hebrew root *nidui*, which means "banishment" or "ostracism." In a way, *niddah* is the perfect word to describe their state. A number of congregants whom I have counseled tell me that when all their friends are starting families, they feel ostracized from their peers, as they are unable to share in the experience of creating a child. They feel they are *niduim*, banished from the status quo. I remember sitting with one member of our congregation who told me that she used to love coming to our synagogue, but now that she is dealing with infertility, she finds it too painful to be in a community that celebrates the children she desperately wants.

My congregants' experience is mirrored in the way our Rabbis see Hannah's struggles, another woman who famously dealt with the shame and loneliness of infertility in the Bible. Like many who have experienced this struggle, Hannah questions her body. In one midrash, she cries out to God, "Master of the universe, all that You created in women, there is not one part without its purpose—eyes to see, ears to hear, a nose to smell, a mouth to speak, hands to work with, legs to walk with, breasts to nurse. But the breasts you placed over my heart—what are they for? Are they to nurse?" (Talmud, *Berachot* 31b). Like Hannah, many who face infertility watch others whose bodies seem to behave normally and ask why it isn't true for them.

The presence of children when we are unable to have one can feel callous and taunting. Just as Rachel had to watch her sister Leah's successful pregnancies, Hannah had to watch her husband Elkanah's other wife Peninah give birth. Unlike Leah, however, who was modest about her pregnancies, Peninah took every opportunity to remind Hannah of her inability to conceive. Our Rabbis imagine that she used to mock Hannah, "Did you buy a sweater for your eldest son?... Did you buy a shirt for your second son?" (*Midrash Samuel* 1:8). In another imagined conversation, Peninah taunted her, "Aren't you going to greet your children when they come home from school?" (*Pesikta Rabbati* 34:8).

Making Infertility Less Invisible

Although Peninah's scorn for Hannah was deliberate and malicious, our words when discussing children in our community can be likewise hurtful. I remember seeing an email from one Jewish group in the Brooklyn area saying, "Everyone is pregnant; come to Shabbat and find out who." Many in our community came forward, angry that an assumption was made that getting pregnant was easy. And though this email was an extreme case, there are other offenses that are much more subtle. Too many communities draw a distinction between "young couples" and "young families," implying that to be taken seriously as a "family" you need children. Likewise, we all too often celebrate births without acknowledging the difficulties associated with having children. It was a real wake-up moment for me when I was told by a congregant that my yearly ritual of blessing families on Rosh Hashanah who had had babies within the past year was the reason she could no longer attend our High Holy Day services. Watching them, there was no catharsis for her. Just pain. Because of her, we started reciting a prayer for those struggling with infertility.

There is no question that each of these struggles drives those who are dealing with infertility away from community and toward isolation. It is lonely when you cannot enter into community because its children cause you pain. It is lonely when others make assumptions about your worth without children. But perhaps most of all, it is lonely dealing with a struggle that is accompanied by so much shame. Years ago, the subject of breast cancer was considered taboo, and women who dealt with it were relegated to struggle in silence. Over the past few decades, breast cancer has become part of the American lexicon, and those who suffer from it are able to speak openly about their struggle. We can do the same with infertility.

The first step in helping those with infertility is to help them realize they are not alone. Many others struggle alongside them, and the Bible can be a model for this. Because Rachel did not have many children of her own, God rewarded her courage by making her the mother of all the Jewish people. However, that would come at a cost. She would suffer alongside her children. After they turned away from God and were punished with the destruction of the Temple, the prophet Jeremiah described Rachel's mourning: "A cry is heard in Ramah—wailing, bitter weeping—Rachel weeping for her children. She refuses to be comforted for her children, who are gone" (Jeremiah 31:15).

Her pain would serve a greater purpose, however. According to the Bible, Rachel died and was buried along the side of the road on the way to Ephrat, near Bethlehem (Genesis 35:19). The Rabbis teach that while Rachel certainly shed tears for the suffering of her children, the Israelites also shed tears when they thought of Rachel. After the destruction of the Temple, the Jews were marched to Babylonia by way of her grave (*Genesis Rabbah* 82:10). As they passed it in their shock and sadness, Rachel prayed for them, and her presence allowed them to cry as well (*Pesikta Rabbati* 3:2). Her pain facilitated a catharsis they so desperately needed at the moment.

It is certainly lonely dealing with infertility, but if our ancestors teach us anything it is that knowing we are suffering alongside another means we aren't necessarily suffering alone.

The Loneliness of Sickness

One of the least discussed stories of loneliness in the Bible is that of King Uzziah. Becoming king at the age of sixteen and reigning for fifty-two years, he was considered a relatively good leader. Throughout his life, "he did what was pleasing to God" (2 Chronicles 26:4). He was an artful builder, a brave and skilled military leader, and a pious worshiper. However, our tradition teaches that despite Uzziah's gifts, he also struggled with arrogance. And it was this flaw that would eventually lead to his downfall.

Although he knew that offering incense to God was the role of the Temple priests, Uzziah refused to accept his limited status. He demanded a turn serving God and forced his way into the holy sanctuary of the Temple. Though the priest Azariah, along with "eighty other brave priests" admonished him, he refused to listen (2 Chronicles

26:17). Soon their protests made him angry. Yet, no sooner did Uzziah let his rage well up than *tzaraat*, a scaly affliction found throughout the Bible, broke out on his forehead. God had caused a plague to come upon him because he did not listen, and he would find no cure. The Bible continues:

> King Uzziah was a leper until the day of his death. He lived in isolated quarters as a leper, for he was cut off from the House of God—while Jotham his son was put in charge of the king's house and governed the people of the land. (2 Chronicles 26:21)

Left with this mysterious disease, caused presumably by his own arrogance, Uzziah was cut off from the world. His sickness would isolate him from all those he knew and loved. One can imagine him, living out his final days in some tower, only able to watch as life went on below without him. No visitors would arrive at his doorstep. He was locked away from all as he prepared for the day of his death. We must imagine that during that time the words of the Torah echoed in his head, a warning to all those who would develop *tzaraat*, "He shall be unclean as long as the disease is on him. Being unclean, he shall dwell apart; his dwelling shall be outside the camp." (Leviticus 13:46).

A Forced Migration

In her book *Illness as Metaphor*, Susan Sontag begins with the observation that "everyone holds dual citizenship, in the kingdom of the well and in the kingdom of the sick."[3] For some, moving from health to sickness is a gradual process. We have time and space to plan. We prepare ourselves and those we love for the eventual move from one kingdom to the other. But for others, it is a forced migration. We are well one day, and the next our lives are turned upside down. We are unmoored by sickness.

As it is for so many, Uzziah was given little warning. In an instant everything about his life changed. Where once he could walk freely among the people, now he was trapped between four walls. Where once he wielded power over others, now he was helpless against the ails of his own body. Where once he was admired by all his subjects, now he was rejected by all but his most basic servants. His isolation and confinement, his alienation and impotence, were all a result of his illness. Sickness had snatched away his power, his status, and his relationships, and it was threatening, as illness often does, to steal away his one remaining possession, his life.

Uzziah's story reminds me of my uncle's struggle with brain cancer. Because of where the tumor was located, tasks that used to be easy suddenly became impossible. At first, walking up the stairs and putting on his shoes became tough. But quickly, the greatest challenges for him became speaking and swallowing. Though he was only in his forties, my uncle watched as in a matter of months his body deteriorated past that of men twice his age.

I can only imagine that stuck inside a body that did not respond to him, my uncle felt trapped. He was like Uzziah, locked in the tower with only a window out to the world where he once thrived. Sontag was right; we all make the transition between the kingdom of the well and the kingdom of the sick. However, there is a one-way mirror between the two kingdoms. Only those who are sick are constantly reminded of what could have awaited them on the other side.

Uzziah's sickness has another factor to it that some who are ill share: he was partly to blame. It's clear from the biblical narrative that had Uzziah not entered into the sanctuary, he would not have gotten sick. Though many do get sick for no apparent reason, there are many illnesses that are explainable. Some smokers get lung cancer and emphysema. Unsafe sexual practices can lead to AIDS. Obesity can cause diabetes, and stress can lead to heart disease. Because of what might have been, each of these illnesses has an added degree of shame and self-loathing attached to it. I've seen so much anger surrounding sickness, but when that anger is turned inward, the alienation of the ill only grows. Self-blame becomes destructive and creates a wall between the afflicted and the rest of the world.

Illness and Death Are Not the Same

Perhaps the most tragic element of Uzziah's illness was the fact that he was treated as if he were dead even before he passed away. Because many people don't want to face their own mortality, being with some-one who is ill is uncomfortable. We look into their faces and are forced to encounter our own frailty and vulnerability. Many of us lack the bravery and self-awareness needed to be with those who suffer, so we disappear. We stop calling and we stop writing. We create distance. Soon the ill are not in our lives anymore. It is as if they no longer exist. Our Rabbis were right when they observed that for someone with *tzaraat*, "it is as if they are already dead" (*Exodus Rabbah* 1:34).

When Uzziah did die, his death would be no better than his life. In his book *How We Die: Reflections on Life's Final Chapter*, Sherwin B. Nuland explains:

> We compose scenarios that we yearn to see enacted by our mortally ill beloved, and the performances are successful just often enough to sustain our expectation. Faith in the possibility of such a scenario has ever been a tradition of Western societies, which in centuries past valued a good death as the salvation of the soul and an uplifting experience for friends and family and cel-ebrated it in the literature and pictorial representations of *ars moriendi*, the art of dying.... The good death has ... been for the most part a myth.[4]

Nuland's words ring true for Uzziah. His sickness was tragic and lacked any semblance of nobility. His death was a gasp in the history of the Jewish people and in his family. Perpetuating that myth only makes the ill wonder why they can't achieve something that rarely exists in the first place.

Even after Uzziah's death, his loneliness would continue. Rather than being buried alongside his ancestors, Uzziah was placed in a grave in a nearby burial field (2 Chronicles 26:23). Since he had been sick at the time of his death, he was impure. Though his deeds deserved a place beside his forebearers, his body did not. In death, Uzziah was cast aside as he was in life. His sickness would condemn him to rest eternally alone.

Not everyone who is ill has the same experience as Uzziah. Many find support in family and friends throughout their ordeal. Many weather their changes in body and mind with dignity and courage. And some even recover. Yet, there is little question that Uzziah's experience of illness, his isolation, his anger, his loneliness, and his invisibility are present in some form in nearly all our sicknesses. The key is to bring these struggles into the open. The ill need not suffer alone in their tower. We may not be able to snap our fingers and magically erase their helplessness and alienation, but we can acknowledge that it exists. Uzziah's story is a powerful reminder that the feelings of the ill are natural, but it is also a warning that we too often act callously and make them feel worse.

The Loneliness of Growing Old

Our ancient Rabbis loved to speculate on the defining feature of each decade of life (*Mishnah Avot* 5:21). Thirty is the year of strength. Forty is the age of understanding. Fifty is the age of counsel. But something happens when we turn sixty, for that year is the year of "old age." And moving forward, each decade gets worse. Seventy is the decade of gray hair; ninety, the decade of the bent back. At one hundred it is as if a person were "dead, passed away, and ceased from the world."[5]

Sadly, not much has changed in the two thousand years since this text was written. It is a lonely experience to age. While today advances in medicine have allowed people to live longer and healthier as they age and there are many who are enjoying the space and fruits of growing old, society still sends the message that the fundamental experience of aging is fraught with challenges: finding purpose in retirement, feeling positive about our previous accomplishments, learning to come to peace with those things we cannot change about the past, and struggling with changes in our body and mind. But perhaps more than anything, there are two paramount and interconnected challenges that our elderly face that lead to loneliness: the loss of their social network and the unfair assumptions that society makes about the elderly based on their age.

Losing Your Social Network

Moses faces both of these challenges as he nears the end of his life. Living to the age of 120, and as one of the last leaders of his generation, Moses is doomed to watch as everyone he knew in his adult life passes away before his eyes. Moses is the ancient equivalent of the aging Ben Whittaker, Robert De Niro's character in the movie *The Intern*, whose weeks are marked by the constant and steady rhythm of funeral announcements, as one by one his social circle dies off and crumbles around him. Moses buries his sister Miriam and his brother Aaron. Every chieftain who accompanied him atop Sinai, every architect who built the desert Tabernacle, die before his eyes.

Besides Joshua and Caleb, to whom he will pass on the mantle of leadership, Moses's only remaining confidant is God. Moses is the only person throughout history who is said to have been able to talk to God "face to face" (Deuteronomy 34:10). However, where once this bond was strong, it does not supersede and override God's decision to punish Moses at the end of his life. There is little agreement about why God marches Moses through the wilderness for forty years only to leave him on the wrong side of the Jordan River, never able to enter the Promised Land with his people. Some authorities say it is because Moses disobeyed God, striking a rock in anger when God told him speak to it.[6] Others explain that God's decision is a retroactive punishment for Moses's idea to send spies into the Land of Israel to scout it, rather than believe that God's plan would work in the first place.[7]

Whatever the reason, Moses's final days are punctuated by constant pleads with God to change this decree.[8] Moses invokes everything he has. Rabbinic stories abound where Moses reminds God of his labors in life (*Deuteronomy Rabbah* 9:8), his leadership of six hundred thousand people (*Deuteronomy Rabbah* 9:9), and his purity of heart (*Deuteronomy Rabbah* 9:10). Nevertheless, God refuses to acquiesce. It is a tragedy that Moses is left with only God to rely on in the end, and yet God cannot be his source of strength in his final days. And without God, Moses has no one.

Finding Meaninglessness in the Past

Moses's loneliness late in life has another insidious layer that many who are forced to retire know all too well. When Moses invokes all his holy deeds and is met with deaf ears, he is given the implicit message that all that he did in the past is irrelevant. As a rabbi, I've seen this play out firsthand in the lives of my congregants. It is nearly impossible to both convey to someone what they meant to a company or community in the past and give them the message they are not needed now. As we work, we can't help but keep score. We stay late one day. We do a favor the next. We pour our soul into this project, nurture wholeheartedly this relationship, all the while assuming we will benefit from our work later. But others do not keep score like we do. When we are let go, it is often because today we are not right for our job. The past becomes irrelevant, but we hold onto it as a source of resentment and anger.[9] By not weighing Moses's past deeds toward a favorable outcome, God severs the final intimate relationship of Moses's old age. Though Jewish tradition would see reconciliation for the two in Moses's final hour— God is said to have taken Moses's soul with a kiss (Talmud, *Bava Batra* 17a)—the strain caused by the dissolution of this relationship would color Moses's final days in a lonely darkness.

Our Unfair Expectations on the Elderly

But more than even God's abandonment, Moses felt acutely the people's contempt. Moses's last days were of personal alienation precisely because of the assumptions that society made about him. True, our tradition tells us that Moses defied expectations of age. He lived to be 120 years old, and his "sight was unimpaired and his vigor had not abated." (Deuteronomy 34:7). In fact, it was said that on the day of his death he was able to leap up to the top of Mount Nebo in one stride (Talmud, *Sotah* 13b). Despite these facts, there were many in his community who did not acknowledge his youthfulness in old age. Like the ancient adage that at the age of one hundred it is as if one were already dead, Moses was treated as such.

There is a strain of Jewish thought that says that because of Moses's age, he lacked the skills to touch future generations. Rabbi Yehuda Aryeh Leib Alter, known to many as the Gerer Rebbe, was one such voice. He did not see Moses's death as a punishment. Instead, it came because Moses was no longer fit to be the kind of leader Israel needed. In his old age, the Gerer Rebbe tells us, Moses had lost touch with the youth.

A new generation needed a new leader, and Moses was too old for the task. A quick glance at the differences between Moses and his successor Joshua shows the differences between these two leaders. Moses has a more direct relationship with God; Joshua, a more indirect one. Moses is apart from the people; Joshua is of the people. Moses has never seen the land; Joshua was one of the scouts who toured the land thirty-eight years previously. In truth Joshua's attributes may have seemed better suited for this next stage of Jewish history. Nevertheless, by being denied his leadership post and subsequent entry into the Promised Land, Moses is told a harsh truth: *the people will do better without you than with you.*

The Implicit Messages We Send

The jury is still out about whether it is true that Moses wasn't needed. The Bible makes it clear that when the people entered the Promised Land, many went astray. After Moses's death, the people certainly faced leadership challenges and struggles. But what is universally true about Moses's story is that he wasn't the last elderly member of our community to be told that the gifts he had to offer were not needed. All too often, we send the message to those oldest among us that younger generations speak a cultural language they cannot learn. By calling today, for example, "the Internet age" and ourselves the "online generation," we make assumptions and exclude those in older generations from being part of our cultural ethos. We all too often make judgments about people's skills, interests, and potential by looking at their birth dates, without getting to know them. We assume someone is too old without first discovering if they are up for the task.

I remember speaking to an elderly member of my congregation who bemoaned the fact when he and his home aide went out, people addressed his aide rather than him. When he went to the hospital with his adult children, his doctor never once spoke directly to him about his own care, choosing instead to engage his sons in conversation. There is little that is more alienating to the self than feeling like you are invisible. When we deny those who are older the humanity they deserve, we send them the message that their existence is not important, a message that can only lead to loneliness.

But if Moses is a symbol of the challenges of growing old, he is also a symbol of comfort. Despite the struggles Moses faced at the end, despite his isolation, despite the fracture he felt among the people, Moses's suffering was remembered. Though his community did not come through for him in the end, history did. Moses is perhaps more relevant today than he was at the moment of his death, and that is in large part because of the humanity he showed in his final days. Moses is a reminder to all those struggling with the challenges of aging that even when we feel invisible and think that others overlook our momentous lives, they are written in the annals of history. Moses shows each aging person who feels lonely that there is something holy in the struggle. It was preserved in the Torah.after all.

PART 2

Loneliness as
the Building Block
of the Jewish Faith

5

Our Lonely God

What the Loneliest Being in the Universe Can Teach Us about Our Suffering

There's a story told that on Rosh Hashanah, a group of angels began celebrating the New Year. They gathered as a group and began to sing a series of praises to God called *Hallel*, giving thanks for another year. But upon hearing their songs, God rebuked them. "I'm sitting here, with the Book of Life open before me, deciding who will live and who will die in the coming year, and you're singing? How could you celebrate at a time like this! From now on, there will be no singing at this time of year" (based on Talmud, *Rosh Hashanah* 32b).

In a season when God is deciding the fate of the world, God has a job that no one, not even the angels in heaven can understand. It is certainly a lonely position. The weight of the world rests on God's shoulders. God must decide who will live and who will die in the coming year, and God is anxious over these life-altering decisions. God can't possibly share in the joy of the angels, so God outlaws it.

If previous chapters taught that it may potentially bring comfort to those suffering from loneliness to know that the feeling is pervasive in our tradition and among our ancestors, then certainly for some, it may bring comfort to know just how deeply the emotion pervades the heavens. While some theologians have seen God as lacking human emotion and form,[1] others see God as sharing and modeling some of the deepest

71

pain in the universe. God is often known in our tradition as the "King of kings," thus God has no equal—no equal in might, no equal in mercy, but also no equal in suffering.

God's loneliness can be seen most clearly at three seminal moments in history: the creation of the world, the giving of the Torah, and the destruction of the First and Second Temples. While each is different, these phases of history combine to paint a picture of a God who is truly suffering, a God in need of companionship who is constantly disappointed by humanity, who take their creator for granted.

The Lonely Creator

One of the fundamental questions of human existence is, why are we here? Why did God create the world? And what is the purpose of humanity? As it turns out, one prominent answer to this question can be summarized by the 1922 poem "Creation" by James Weldon Johnson:

> And God stepped out on space,
> And He looked around and said,
> "I'm lonely—
> I'll make me a world."[2]

Whether he knew it or not, Johnson, a Christian writer and activist, was in fact stating a fundamental truth about the birth of the world: God was in need of companionship, so our creator created.

Over the course of six days, God created everything we know. God created heaven and earth, the sky, the sea, the sun, and the moon. God created animals, plants, fish, and birds. But despite all of these creations, God did not feel any less lonely.

Even the angels in heaven did not help God's alienation. There is little agreement on the role of angels in the universe, yet one consistent theme arises: angels have the unique job of serving God. In fact, according to one midrash, God creates a choir of angels every day whose sole task is to sing God's praises (Talmud, *Chagigah* 14a). In another teaching, God creates a special set of angels known as the *chayyot*, whose primary purpose is to hold up the divine holy throne.[3] In fact, God is rarely alone. Psalm 82:1 teaches that "God stands in the divine assembly, among the divine beings" and among these masses of angels "pronounces judgment" on the world.

Yet, as it is well known and as we have established, crowds do not mean community, and company does not always bring comfort. Despite the fact that God was rarely alone, heaven did not serve its most important purpose: God did not feel any less lonely. God would need to create human beings in order to accomplish this.

God Needs Humanity to Be Seen

There are countless midrashim that explain why God created humanity. In one we learn that after creating the animals, God took the angels around to name each species (*Genesis Rabbah* 17:4). Though these angels could speak to God and sing God's praises, they lacked a fundamental feature of humanity: they did not embody creativity. These angels could not find the words to describe the creatures they saw around them. When God created humanity, he took Adam around. Adam subsequently named each animal, but he did not stop there. After he had named each creature in the garden, Adam turned to himself and proclaimed he was to be called Adam, for he had come from the earth (*adamah*). Then Adam did something surprising. He turned to his creator and gave God a name as well. That day God formally adopted the name *Adonai*. True, the angels had sung praises to God, but it was Adam who could see God enough to give God a name and an identity. Through Adam, God would become less invisible.

The idea embodied in this midrash is that God tasked humanity not just with populating the earth,[4] but with cultivating a relationship with the Divine. That relationship was rooted in their ability to see and name God. As a rabbi, I often feel the power of names and live the consequences of forgetting them. When most congregants complain about the approachability of a clergy member or the warmth of a community, their first critique is that no one knows their name. Names are packages for identity. Using someone's name conveys familiarity and intimacy. Knowing someone's name is a first and necessary step to discovering the individual's story. Because of this, we hold our names quite dear. Studies have shown that more than perhaps any other word in our lexicon, we can most easily identify our own name. Psychologists call this the "cocktail party effect," because although we are able to tune out nearly every other conversation in a crowded room, we tend to easily overhear and get distracted by the mention of our name, even from far away.

The angels could not name God. They were masters of speaking *about* God. But without the facility of God's name, they could not speak *to* the Divine. They would forever be dancing around God's identity, not focusing in on it. That would be our job.

Perhaps more than naming God, humanity was to feel called and able to speak that name aloud. According to one midrash, before the world was created there was chaos. Storms raged and blew primordial water across the deep. As the water flowed, it emitted faint praises to God (*Lamentations Rabbah* 1:52).[5] Hearing that praise, God was unimpressed. "If these waters, which have no mouth, tongue, utterance, or speech, praise me," said God, "how much the more so if I were to create human beings!" To explain God's decision, the midrash likens the waters to a kingdom of deaf-mutes who praise God with gestures and God to a king. "If these mute subjects praise me thus, how much the more so those who can speak." The king then fills his palace with those subjects who are adept at speaking. Through humanity, God would live out the cocktail party effect. God would hear the divine name across the cosmos, faint and far away, but close enough to register that it was still relevant.

Our Sins Banish God

Sadly, a learned student of the Bible knows that God does not always achieve symbiosis with humanity. We humans consistently disappoint God. The midrash continues that after the king replaced the deaf-mutes with the gift of gab, they rebelled: "They arose and seized the king's palace, saying, 'This palace belongs to nobody but us!'" Likewise, humanity, now endowed with the ability to be in deep relationship with God, failed in that task. We know the stories. Adam and Eve eat the forbidden fruit despite God's insistence that they abstain. Cain kills his brother Abel, and when confronted by God, he lies about knowing anything of his brother's fate. A few chapters later, the world becomes filled with licentiousness and hate, and God must choose, in the generation of Noah, to destroy it and start again.

During each of these events, our Rabbis teach, God drew further away from our world (*Genesis Rabbah* 19:7). God's true home is here on earth with us. But after Adam's sin, God left the comfort of earth and migrated to the first layer of heaven, displaying physically the distance between the creator and earth's creations. After Cain's sin, God moved further from us into the second layer. Each subsequent sin of humanity would banish God farther from home, until many generations later, God would sit alone in the seventh circle of heaven, yearning to return. It would take many generations of righteous individuals to bring God back to earth. God would need Abraham, Isaac, Levi, Amram, and Moses, among others, to bring righteousness into the world and invite God back to stand beside humanity.

The motif of God fleeing the world is only exacerbated in another audacious teaching from our Rabbis (*Tanchuma, Naso* 4). In this midrash, they write that as long as God's presence fills the universe, no one would have the space to sin. We do not have the strength to break God's rules in God's midst. Yet, when sinners, like thieves or adulterers, seek to sin, they banish God from before their presence, giving themselves a vacuum to engage in their illicit behavior. "Go away for an hour," they exclaim, and because God is filled with mercy, God does, shrinking away. In a single moment, the sinners have communicated to God something that is truly hurtful: I would rather live in a world without You. When this happens, God faces a choice. Will God destroy them for sinning or leave as they have asked, giving them the opportunity to repent later? Naturally, God leaves but not before hearing the sinners' message loud and clear: You are not important to me. We can only imagine the alienation and loneliness that saturate this hour of divine exile and the pain felt by God, who is forced to watch earth's children err.

Over and over, humanity challenges God. The exact people who were intended to see God, to mimic the ways of the Divine, and to speak their creator's name time and again default on that opportunity. There is an ancient belief that humanity was created to be God's partner in creation (*Tanchuma, Tazria* 7). In fact, God left a little bit of the world unfinished for us to perfect alongside our Creator. In a way, this teaching is similar to the way some parents leave a small section of yard work undone when their children are little. Knowing it might be too much for small children to spend the whole afternoon working, they call out when nearly finished. That way, they and their children both have a sense of accomplishment when the last weeds are pulled or the last leaves bagged. Similarly, God wanted to share in the accomplishment of creation with us. God and humanity could together look around at the world, and God would say, "Look what we did together!"

Too often in our history, humanity flees from this opportunity and, by turning away from God, makes God more lonely than if they had not been created in the first place. No one wants to hear no. No one wants to feel dismissed. And God is no different. To ask for another to see you is a vulnerable thing indeed. This is precisely the reason most people avoid asking for love and support in the first place. Yet, God asked for support. God sought a relationship with us. When we turn a blind eye, the pain of losing us and the agony of our rejection may in fact have hurt more than our absence from the world in the first place. For if God is anything like us, the pain of loss often outweighs the benefits of gain by a factor of two.[6] Or to put it another way, the pain when someone turns his or her back on you overshadows the joy when a number of people reach out.

In creating humanity, God reached out saying, "Be My partners. Speak My name. Be in relationship with Me." But we did not heed the call. The story of humanity is the saga of a people spurning their creator while God hopes that next time will yield a better result. Yet, the farther we get into history, and the more God gives to humanity, the easier it is to alienate God, especially when God gives heaven's greatest treasure, the Torah, to Israel and they rebuff the gift.

The Loneliness of Sinai

There is a tradition that God created the Torah before the world was in existence. It was God's greatest treasure and the blueprint through which God created the universe (*Genesis Rabbah* 1:1). More than perhaps anything else in the cosmos, God valued the Torah, which made it all the more special when God was ready to give it away.

Yet, our tradition tells us that God could not find anyone to take it. There is a midrash that God went around to every nation of the world, hoping to give them the gift of Torah, but as each read it, they all found something to reject (*Lamentations Rabbah*, proem 24). One nation did not like the prohibition against incest and told God to leave them alone. Another did not want the Torah because of its prohibition against murder. Eventually there was only Israel left to accept God's teaching and law.

Naturally, after these series of rejections one might imagine that God was worried no one would accept this gift. Many know this feeling. We have something that has such significance to us, be it a passion, ideal, or story that we want to share with others. Eventually, we get up the courage to try, but still no one responds. This kind of rejection is toxic. It makes us question so many fundamental truths we see about ourselves. When our gifts are turned away, we blame ourselves. Rather than see situational factors as the reason for others' rejection, we assign the blame inward. Our gifts are defective and thus unwanted.

It is no wonder then that according to one midrash, after freeing the Israelites from slavery in Egypt and leading Israel to the foot of Mount Sinai, God coerces Israel into accepting the Torah (Talmud, *Shabbat* 88a). Our Rabbis teach that God uproots the mountain, turning it over like an inverted cask above their heads. "If you will accept My Torah, all will be fine and good," says God, "but if you do not, I will let go and this will be your grave."

Combining these stories conveys a clear narrative: God is afraid that yet again another group of people will reject the Torah. Israel is God's last hope. Each rejection has built up anger and resentment. God is insecure, and anger and ire are the protection God builds to shelter the Self. We all know people who have reached this stage. Setback upon setback has built a protective coating around their ego. Their self-worth is held up by a fine string. Afraid someone may come to cut it, they surround it with aggression, rage, and indignation. Then, the next time they must ask for something, afraid of yet again being disappointed, they come into the conversation with guns blazing, ready for fight. "I'll make sure you don't say no like the others," says God, "so I'll make you an offer you can't refuse."

And Israel does say yes. They stand proudly at the foot of Sinai and proclaim that they will do and heed all that is in the Torah. Yet, this action does little to alleviate God's pain. Since the creation of the world, God has relied on the companionship of the Torah. Like a trusted advisor whose presence calms and sustains, the Torah has been the most steadfast presence in God's universe. Giving the Torah away would be one of the hardest things God would do. It would be God's great gamble. If humanity would embrace the Torah's teachings and live out its values, God's sacrifice would be worth it. If Israel scorns the Torah, the sacrifice would be for naught, and God would be left to watch from a lonely distance as the Jewish people reject God's most precious gift.

God's trepidation around the giving of the Torah can be seen in perhaps the most tender midrash about revelation. Soon after giving the book to the Jewish people, God instructs Moses, "Let them make Me a sanctuary that I may dwell among them" (Exodus 25:8). This command kicks off perhaps the greatest building project of Jewish history, the construction of the *Mishkan* (Tabernacle), God's dwelling place in the desert and the precursor to the Holy Temple in Jerusalem. The *Mishkan* would be the space where God would talk to the Israelites and where they would make sacrifices to the Divine. But why build the structure in the first place?

Our tradition compares God's request to build the Tabernacle to that of a king whose only daughter gets married. Speaking to his future son-in law, the king says:

> "My daughter, whose hand I have given you, is my only child. I cannot part with her, but neither can I say to you, 'Do not take her,' because she is now your wife. One favor, however, I request of you: Wherever you go to live, prepare a chamber for me that I may dwell with you, for I cannot leave my daughter." Thus God

said to Israel, "I have given you a Torah from which I cannot part, and I also cannot tell you not to take it. But this I ask: wherever you go, make for Me a house where I may sojourn," as it says, "Let them make Me a sanctuary that I may dwell among them" (Exodus 25:8). (*Exodus Rabbah* 33:1)

Our tradition sees God as a concerned father dealing with an empty nest. Will Israel treat their gift well? And moreover, what will God do when lonely? In this moment of transition, God hopes there will be a place beside Israel to come visit from time to time.

Scorning God's Gift

No sooner does God give the gift of the Torah than Israel commits a twofold rejection. First, the Jewish people build the golden calf, worshiping it rather than their faceless God. Looking out at the mass of people led by Aaron, God is rightfully enraged. If the giving of the Torah was a marriage between God and the Jewish people, as some commentaries see it, then our Rabbis are right in reminding us, "Shameless is the bride who plays the harlot while still under the wedding canopy" (Talmud, *Shabbat* 88b). God is the scorned husband, whose lover has run into the arms of another, and it is only natural that immediately upon finding out about Israel's construction of the golden calf, God would cry out to Moses, who is standing beside his creator on the mountain when the news arrives. However, God's cry is not one in search of support. Rather than asking for Moses's comfort, God asks for his absence: "Leave Me alone that My anger may blaze forth against them and that I may destroy them" (Exodus 32:10, translation mine).

While the incident of the golden calf is certainly a pox on our collective Jewish history—it is said that each generation is punished residually at least in part for the sin of the golden calf (*Exodus Rabbah* 43:2)—there is a voice in our tradition that sees the incident as helping to alleviate God's loneliness. At the moment that God cries out, Moses responds. There is a peculiarity in the aftermath of the golden calf that our Rabbis identify. They are surprised that God needs to ask Moses to be left alone (*Exodus Rabbah* 42:9). Why wouldn't God just leave the mountain if God wanted to sit in solitude? Hadn't God done this in previous eras of history, such as God's escape to heaven after Adam and Eve ate the forbidden fruit?[7] Their answer is that "Leave me alone" is actually a cry for help. They liken God to a king whose son sins. Taking him into a chamber to punish him, the king cries, "Leave me alone, leave me alone," hoping that someone will hear him. Walking by, his son's teacher hears the king's plea and approaches the king. He saves the son but also lets the king know that he is there for him. So, too, does God cry out for Moses to listen in this moment of pain, and Moses responds, not leaving the mountain until God calms down and they come to a resolution. In fact, in another somewhat audacious midrash, the Rabbis read the words "leave Me alone" (*hanichah li*) as "let go of Me" and imagine that Moses is grabbing hold of God, advocating for Israel, while at the same time drawing God close and reminding his creator that he is still here (Talmud, *Berachot* 32a).[8]

Walking Away from God's Mountain

Although Moses does much to let God know he is not alone after the golden calf incident, Israel shows God the opposite after the ordeal is finished. In the eyes of our Rabbis, the first sin, committed by the people after Sinai is the way in which Israel walks away from the mountain (Talmud, *Shabbat* 115b–116a). When describing the Israelites' movement away from Sinai, the Torah (Numbers 10:33) uses the words *Vayisu mehar Adonai*, often translated as "And they [the Israelites] marched from the mountain of God." However, the Rabbis see the opaque phrase as meaning "And they turned away from following God." Expounding on this more, a group of rabbis known as the *Tosafot* tell us that the Israelites fled the mountain like "a child fleeing from school," knowing that God (i.e., their teacher) had already given them so many commandments and hoping if they ran away fast enough they would not have to accept any more.[9]

We can only imagine the pain this simple and childish act causes God. Israel has become a bully, and God their victim. God is left wholly alone on Sinai and utterly abandoned by the people. The saga of the golden calf can be explained away: the Israelites did not understand the implications of the Torah's law against idol worship, and out of fear they built an idol that would anger God. Yet, there is no way to explain their fleeing. The people do not value God's laws. God's precepts are a nuisance, and the Israelites lack the decency to convey that notion to God directly. They value their relationship with God so little that they run away. A people who God once proclaimed "treasured" (Exodus 19:5) just played playground politics with their creator. There can be no greater shock.

From then on Israel would continue to err before God. There would be rebellions, nostalgia for Egypt, and murmurings against Moses. But the worst sin of all would be the decision not to trust that God will protect them when they enter the Promised Land. Instead, the people trust ten spies who are sent ahead and who report that they stand no chance against the natives, who look like "giants" (Number 13:32). They allow fear to govern their settlement decisions. At each stage during their journey in the desert, and through mistake after mistake, these actions are seen as slights against God, alienating God more and proving that humanity could not cure God's loneliness.

God's Lonely Decision: The Destruction of the Temple

The greatest of all trespasses occurs in the years leading up to 586 BCE and eventually lead to God's decision to destroy the Holy Temple in Jerusalem. There is little agreement among commentators about what Israel did that forced God to choose this punishment for them. According to some accounts, the sins included not studying the commandments, scorning those who perform them, hating teachers, and denying their divine origin. Yet, perhaps worst of all was the act of denying God's existence.[10]

There is a childhood game that many have experienced. A group of children decide collectively to ignore another child. The victim speaks, but no one responds. They act as if the other child is dead, a ghost beyond perception. The reason this game is so maddening is because we see ourselves through the eyes of others. Our worth is measured by the way others interact with us. We know we are funny or smart because we are told so. Though Descartes said, "I think, therefore I am," he was wrong. When others deny our existence, we lose our sense of self. We may think, but we exist, we are, because others allow us to be. So too, when we collectively deny God's existence, we alienate God from Godself, a lonely state indeed.

Yet, God's alienation only got worse as God sought to warn Israel of their sins. According to Rabbinic lore, as Israel's sins worsened, God backed slowly out of the Temple, hoping they would notice that the divine presence was missing (*Lamentations Rabbah*, proem 25). God moved from the holy sanctuary, out the door, through the gate, eventually landing on the Mount of Olives. God moved ten steps in all, but at no point did Israel see they were without the Divine. The midrash continues that God spent three and a half years outside of the gates of the Temple on the Mount of Olives, issuing forth a warning daily from heaven: "Turn back, rebellious children" (Jeremiah 3:14); "Turn back to Me, and I will turn back to you" (Malachi 3:7). Here too, God is invisible. No one heeds God's warning, because no one notices it. It's a sorry day indeed when you realize that no one notices your absence because they did not register your presence in the first place.

Eventually, God makes the heart-wrenching decision to destroy the Temple. Our Rabbis explain that knowing how difficult it will be to watch His palace go up in flames, God ties His right hand behind His back, symbolizing a desire to become powerless and ensuring that He would not save the Jewish people at the last minute (*Lamentations Rabbah*, proem 24). Yet, no sooner is the deed done than God realizes the error of that action.

Searching for Space to Mourn

The Jewish tradition has multiple accounts of the aftermath of the Temple's destruction, but there are two that are particularly devastating. In one (*Lamentations Rabbah* 1:1), God summons the ministering angels and asks them, "If a human king had a son who died and mourns for him, what is customary for him to do?" They first respond that he hangs sackcloth on his door. God immediately does this. God asks again, and they tell him to extinguish the heavenly lamps. God immediately does this. Eventually, God follows all of their instructions. God overturns his couch, removes his shoes and walks barefoot, rends his purple robe, sits in silence, and eventually begins to weep and sob. Here, our Rabbis imagine that God has no outlet for his pain. As a divine being, God has never faced something as hard as the destruction of the Temple and the exile of the Jewish people. God is lost and needs to mimic humanity to develop a rite for mourning. Like the human mourners of previous chapters, our tradition imagines God as feeling all the same isolating emotions. Here the angels are helpful in giving him rituals.

However, the angels are not always understanding. Perhaps the most heartbreaking account of God's suffering occurs when God is denied the ability to mourn (*Lamentations Rabbah*, proem 24). God begins crying in heaven, "I am now like a man who had an only son for whom he prepared a marriage canopy but he died under it. Don't you feel sad for me and my children?"[11] Hearing God cry, one of the chief angels in heaven, the Metatron, comes and falls on his face before God. Looking at the Holy One of Blessing, he says, "Sovereign of the universe let me weep, but You should not weep." In Metatron's mind, tears and sobbing are not befitting the Almighty. But God will not be deterred, "If you don't let Me weep now," God replies, "I will repair to a place that you do not have permission to enter and will weep there."

For Metatron, it is not dignified to have God crying. Yet, like any mourner, God needed the space to emote. Sadly, all too often, like God, when we mourn we are not given that space. Just as God is told to remain strong for the universe, we are told to remain strong for our children or to push through our pain to meet others' expectations. Our bosses give us a few weeks of slack and wonder why our work is suffering three months after losing a parent. Our spouses are concerned when nearly a year after losing a sibling we still wake up with grief dreams. God was denied the space to fully grieve, so God took it, threatening Metatron, saying, "I will disappear unless you let Me cry." It's a lonely statement to have to make, and sadly a sentiment many of us do not have space to convey.

However, there is an account put forth by Rabbi Kalonymus Kalman Shapira, one of the rabbis of the Warsaw Ghetto, who said that God did weep in secret. He explains that the reason the world was not destroyed by God's grieving was that God did retire to the innermost chamber of heaven. If God's grief had entered into the world, the universe would have ceased to exist.[12] Here, we can imagine the pain and responsibility that burdened God. God had to choose between seeking others for comfort while putting the world at jeopardy or seeking isolation to preserve existence. According to Rabbi Shapira, God chose loneliness for the greater good.

Our tradition imagines God remaining in that state of mourning since the day of the Temple's destruction. Many disasters have befallen the Jewish people in its history. The Temple was rebuilt and destroyed yet again. Throughout our exile, foreign powers have sought Israel's destruction. All along, God mourns beside us. Until the Temple is rebuilt, our tradition sees God still racked with suffering over the decision to destroy our holiest abode. Rabbi Isaac ben Samuel teaches in the Talmud:

> The night has three [heavenly] watches, and at each watch the Holy One, blessed be He, sits and roars like a lion and says: Woe to the children, on account of whose sins I destroyed My house and burnt My temple and exiled them among the nations of the world. (*Berachot* 3a)

Here, our Rabbis see God continually engaged in a ritual of pain. Heavenly nights are divided into three, and at each stage, God begins it by crying out. While today many of us mention the destruction of the Temple in our prayers without really mourning it, God continues to weep acutely. In fact, in one heart-wrenching tale, Rabbi Nathan enters the Temple area and finds the last remaining wall, the Kotel (the Western Wall), standing. At first he criticizes God for allowing the Temple to be destroyed. But in no time, he hears a response. A voice calls out, telling him to press his ring against the wall. Through the ring, Rabbi Nathan feels the wall trembling. Immediately, his eyes are opened and he realizes why. God is standing above him atop the wall, bowing down and straightening, trembling and weeping (*Tanna D'Vei Eliyahu*

30). To this day, Jewish folklore assumes at least a part of God remains at that wall, and if you pay attention you can still hear the echo of God's mourning inside the ancient Kotel stones.

Suffering Alongside Us Today

Though these stories clearly imagine God as racked with suffering over the aftermath of our exile, God is also burdened with pain over our present sufferings. Said Rabbi Meir, "When a person is in distress, what does God say? 'My head weighs Me down, My arm weighs Me down" (Talmud, *Sanhedrin* 46a). Here, Meir ascribes a familiar emotional phenomenon to God. Suffering can feel heavy and can hurt. This is the reason that people often say depression is accompanied by physical pain. Though humanity is the one suffering, God feels such empathy that human pain is magnified and transmitted into the cosmos. If each person's suffering is a world unto itself, it's a wonder that compounded, any being, even God, could bear it.

In another beautiful teaching, our Rabbis imagine God and the Jewish people as twins (*Exodus Rabbah* 2:5). Just as when the head of one twin aches the other also feels it, God too feels the pain of the Jewish people and whispers from the cosmos, "I am with him in trouble" (Psalm 91:15). For this reason, God seeks out ways to suffer alongside us. When, for example, Israel found itself enslaved in Egypt, God chose a burning thornbush as the place to reveal the Divine to Moses. "Do you realize that I live in trouble, just as Israel lives in trouble?" God said to Moses. "Know that from the place where I am speaking to you—from a thornbush—that I am, as it were, a partner in their trouble [*shotef b'zaaran*]" (*Exodus Rabbah* 2:5). For anyone who has ever found themselves stuck in a pricker bush, the metaphor is apt. God seeks out personal suffering, dwelling in a painful bush, as a symbolic way of showing empathy to a people who suffer. Sadly, humanity does not return the sentiment. They do not suffer beside God.

God's Lonely Search

Many know the saying "You are only as happy as your least happy child." If that is indeed the case, then our tradition sees God as bearing the burden of every loss, every failure, every persecution, and every tragedy. And because as long as there is humanity, there will be suffering, there is no reprieve in sight. So God goes on weeping alongside us. But God is not seen suffering. We have no indication that the cosmos is crying. We do not recognize God's suffering, and consequently God receives no support for it. When we hurt, we can turn to one another. We can even reach out to God. But to whom can God turn?

Hasidic thought sees humanity as fulfilling the central role of seeking out God, who is hiding from us and needs to be found but who would not ask us directly for that support. In one particular tale we hear the story of Rabbi Baruch's grandchild who was playing hide-and-seek with another boy:

> He hid himself and stayed in his hiding place for a long time, assuming that his friend would look for him. Finally, he went out and saw that his friend was gone, apparently not having looked for him at all, and that his own hiding had been in vain. He ran into the study of his grandfather, crying and complaining about his friend. Upon hearing the story, Rabbi Baruch broke into tears and said: "God, too says: 'I hide but there is no one to look for me.'"[13]

Perhaps more than anyone, this sentiment is found in the writings of the twentieth-century theologian Rabbi Abraham Joshua Heschel, whose work *God in Search of Man* saw God as continually calling out to humanity, waiting for our reply. In the Garden of Eden, soon after Adam and Eve have eaten the forbidden fruit, God calls out the one word that will echo through the ages: *Ayekah*, "Where are you?" (Genesis 3:9). "Religion," writes Heschel, "consists of God's question and man's answer."[14] Since creation, God has experienced pain and alienation. Humanity was to be the remedy for God's suffering, but we have consistently fallen short. As Heschel observes, our history with God is punctuated by moments of God calling out, searching for us and hoping we will answer. But we have failed. God called out after creation, but we missed it. God called out at Sinai, and we squandered it. God cried out hoping we would change our ways while the Temples were standing but was forced to punish the Jewish people with their destruction because we did not answer God's entreaty.

True, our tradition sees moments of compassionate presence on the part of humanity. We show God compassion daily during prayer. According to one teaching, when we respond with the words "May God's name be blessed" in our daily prayers, God feels that we have listened to the divine call and has a brief moment of joy, proclaiming publicly the exuberance of being acknowledged, "Happy is the king who is thus praised in this house!" (Talmud, *Berachot* 3b). But perhaps most powerful of all is the image, put forth by our Rabbis, that occurred after God destroyed the Temple and, feeling lonely, went searching for support. God called out and found a group of professional human mourners, commissioned by heaven. In an instant they joined together to mourn alongside God, so that God might feel less lonely (*Lamentations Rabbah*, proem 2). "Call for the mourning women," God cried. "Let them quickly start a wailing *for us*" (Jeremiah 9:16–17, translation and emphasis mine). They will mourn *for us*, said God, since we are both in pain and we will be mourning together. At that moment, God felt less alone. But as we have established, these moments are rare indeed.

6

Israel, the Lonely People

How a Nation Can Suffer Alongside Us

The Bible tells the story of the prophet Balaam, who was sent on a mission from the evil king Balak to curse the Israelites. Rather than curse us, however, Balaam blesses us. At the moment when he opens his mouth for his imprecation, words of love pour forth, part of which reads:

> As I see them from the mountain tops,
> Gaze on them from their heights,
> There is a people that dwells apart,
> Not reckoned among the nations.
>
> (NUMBERS 23:9)

There are few images as lonely as "a people that dwells apart." Isolation is not restricted to human beings or to God. Sometimes a whole people can face loneliness. Throughout the Jewish tradition, there are countless examples of the Jewish people's desertion and derision both by others and by God. We are pariahs to society and overlooked by the Divine. But as we will see, the power of being part of the Jewish people is that our community is built around these struggles. Our community is forged by our shared alienation. We stand alone, together.

Israel and Divine Abandonment

Every conflict has two narratives. If the last chapter spoke of God's alienation from the divine/human encounter, this chapter will speak to ours. Much of human history has been our yearning for divine connection. Yet, throughout time, this special bond has proved unstable. The cosmic connection between God and us is not a love story. It shares more in common with the tales of Eve and Hagar; distance and estrangement are its hallmarks.

Our distance from God began at the very outset. God cast us out of the Garden of Eden and positioned an angel at its entrance to keep us in our exile. Years later, we tried to build a tower to God, and God confounded our speech, scattering us about the earth. Soon, the emblematic Jewish encounter with God would be marked by violence. Left alone, hopelessly lonely, Jacob would fight with God on the banks of the Yabok River. In that struggle he would receive a new name, Israel, "he who strives with God." The Jewish people, named for Jacob, would forge their identity through wrestling, an act of distancing rather than unity.

Eventually we would find our way into Egypt, crying out to a God that it seemed would not answer us. When God did respond and freed us from bondage, our time spent wandering in the desert would be marred by distance and doubt. The Israelites built the golden calf not out of a desire to please God but out of necessity; God was distant and enigmatic, and they believed an idol would bring God close.

Even moments of revelation, the giving of the Torah at Sinai, the command to build the Tabernacle and bring God into our midst, were glimpses rather than gazes of the Divine. There is truth in God's answer to Moses when he asked God to see the divine face. When presented with Moses's yearning to look directly at his creator, God answered Moses, "You cannot see My face, for no one may see Me and live" (Exodus 33:20). Instead, said God, "you will see My back" (Exodus 33:23). The Jewish people are forever looking for a part of God they will not see and settling for a part of God they did not ask for.

Perhaps the loneliest moment in Jewish history came not in the desert, but after the destruction of the Temple. For the Jewish people, the Temple in Jerusalem served a central role. It was the place where God dwelled, an abode of intimacy that they knew had the fingerprints of the Divine. Through sacrifice and worship, they could be close to God. The Temple would give them a mark to direct their prayers and an address for heavenly connection.

Our Rabbis remind us that after the Temple was destroyed, God's presence left the Temple Mount (*Lamentations Rabbah*, proem 29). Though we are reminded time and again in our daily prayers that "due to our sins we were exiled from our land," self-blame did not alleviate our sense of abandonment. Instead it exacerbated our alienation; after the Temple was destroyed, we added ourselves to the list of parties at whom our people could become angry and from whom estranged. For this reason, the metaphor most apt for the experience of losing the Temple was that of divorce.

However, this divorce was of an unorthodox kind. The point of a Jewish divorce is to grant both parties the freedom to move on after a relationship fails. The Torah calls the divorce document, the *get*, a *sefer k'ritut*, literally a "document of cutting off" (Deuteronomy 24:1). A divorce dissolves the ties that bind two people together. It is a great unwinding of destinies that were once merged.

After the Temple was destroyed, God disappeared, moving out of the house and setting off, apart from the Jewish people. Unlike most divorces, however, we were not free when the dust settled. God remained our God. The other nations remained strange and foreign. Left with this reality, our Rabbis were forced to reframe the great divorce.

Two of the most audacious and indicting texts ever written about God address this tension. Both texts see God through the metaphor of a king who becomes disillusioned with his wife. In one account, a king (i.e., God) casts his wife out but reminds her that she is not to interact with her neighbors (*Lamentations Rabbah* 1:56). He fears she might fall in love with them and thus be led toward their practices. "Borrow nothing from them, and lend them nothing," he warns. However, the queen cannot abide by his warning. She is homeless and is forced to go door-to-door, begging for food. After a number of unsuccessful attempts, she returns home to seek reconciliation and finds her husband irate. She did not listen to him, and he is unwilling to take her back. The story ends with a reminder about the injustice done to the queen; either she obeys her husband's command and starves or she disobeys it and loses him. Both options result in disaster.

So too, continue our Rabbis, does Israel struggle after the destruction of the Temple. They wander in exile, unable to fully engage with the world around them, but far from the God that forces their alienation. They are stuck between two impossible alternatives, with nowhere to turn for help.

In another difficult midrash, the Rabbis liken the Jewish people to an *agunah*, a woman who is stuck between marriage and divorce because her husband refuses to give her a *get*. In many cases, an *agunah* watches as her husband exploits a legal loophole in Jewish law; he is permitted to remarry but withholds the document that would allow her the freedom to do so. To make matters worse, in many cases her husband also refuses to provide for her. She gets neither the freedom of divorce nor the financial support of marriage. In the Rabbinic imagination, God is such a husband:

> The Rabbis said: It may be likened to a king who was angry with his consort and wrote out a *get* but got up and snatched it from her. Whenever she wished to remarry, he said to her, "Where is your *get*?" and whenever she demanded her alimony, he said to her, "But have I not divorced you?" Similarly, whenever Israel wished to practice idolatry, the Holy One, blessed be He, said to them, "Where is the bill of your mother's divorce?" (Isaiah 50:1); and whenever they wished that He should perform miracles for them as formerly, the Holy One, blessed be He, said to them, "Have I not already divorced you?" Thus it is written, "I had put her away and given her a bill of divorcement" (Jeremiah 3:8). (*Lamentations Rabbah* 1:3)

According to both texts, the Jewish people are a people trapped. They are unable to free themselves from God but unable to benefit from that connection. They float between. They are forever caught in a tug of war between divine scorn and divine indifference. Even when God seems to care, our Rabbis lack trust. They liken God to a father who had a son. When the boy wept, he placed him on his knees. He wept again, and he took him in his arms. Still he cried, and he put him on his shoulder. Each moment we yearned and God listened, bringing us higher and closer. But in an instant, they say, the son made a mess upon the father. He was too young. He had an accident, and the father threw him forcefully to the ground (*Lamentations Rabbah* 2:2).

Our sages knew how quickly it could feel as if God might turn on us. They lived in a tough world. Jewish history has been no picnic. On a societal level, we have faced persecution, forced conversions, and wars. On a personal level, we deal with death, disease, and suffering. Whether God indeed does play a role in these tragedies is beside the point. Each moment of hardship feels to us that God has abandoned humanity. We stand in the footsteps of our ancestors, facing the same calamities. We weep at our suffering alongside those before us. If the destruction of the Temple is the emblematic low point for our people, then it stands as a symbol of all our struggles; each of our tragedies is a microcosm of it. Whenever we face the dark periods of our lives, it feels as though God has disappeared. Yet, as a people we are not given the luxury to abandon God or our faith. We are trapped, alone in the dungeon of our communal misfortune, crying out to a God who does not answer but who refuses to let us leave.

The Lonely Search for Truth

If the Jewish people could not be close to God, then at least through study we might find ourselves near God's teaching. Throughout Jewish history, our ancestors have yearned to connect to Torah. Yet, at each stage, the study of Torah has left our people wanting. Our learning has brought us close to truth and knowledge, God and revelation, but despite our proximity to these, our study has also uncovered an important fundamental reality: closeness is not connection. The closer we have come to religious truth, the more we have doubted we will ever attain it. The study of Torah, rather than alleviating our loneliness, risks increasing it.

Throughout time, our Rabbis sought to develop metaphors for seeking religious truth. For some, the study of Torah was akin to the search for water when we are parched (Talmud, *Bava Kamma* 82a). For others, it was the yearning of a child for a mother's breast (Talmud, *Eruvin* 54b). Perhaps the most famous metaphor was that of a lover, longing for sexual connection. Our Rabbis compare the learner in the hour of study to a gazelle making love to his mate (ibid.). There is even a story in our Talmud that Rabbi Eleazar ben Padat would study naked, learning Torah in euphoric ecstasy on the streets of Tziporri (ibid.).

The problem with each of these metaphors is that they show us that with Torah study, satisfaction and satiation are temporary. The thirst returns. The hunger arrives. The longing continues. No one is able to fully achieve the knowledge they seek. In fact, even if we could memorize the whole of Torah and every page of Talmud, our learning would still be inadequate. Our Rabbis believed there were different levels to our knowledge. On the surface, we all have access to the plain meaning of our Torah, known as *p'shat*. Each of us can identify where Abraham was born or what Moses said to Pharaoh. On the other end of the spectrum, there are secret meanings to the universe contained in the words of our sacred tradition, known as *sod* (secret). This is esoteric revelation, hidden facts about the nature of God and the heavens.

Our mystics believed that we could periodically glimpse at this knowledge. We could study and meditate and for an instant know a piece of the Divine. We could perceive how the universe was structured, unearth God's motivations, and ascertain heavenly patterns. But sadly, as quickly as these items were revealed, they would disappear.

One of the loneliest images in all of Jewish mysticism involves the struggle to encounter these secrets. In the *Zohar* (*Saba D'Mishpatim* 2:99a), the search for Torah knowledge is likened to a lover gazing into a tower where there lies a hidden maiden. When most people pass, they do not see her, but this lover knows the time when she will reveal herself. As he approaches the palace, she opens a window for him, giving him a glimpse of her visage, and then disappears immediately. As profound as that moment of connection is, it is wanting. She is forever separated from him behind a window. He will never look contentedly into her eyes, never touch her, never hold her. His interactions with her are relegated to momentary acknowledgments.

We seek comfort from our loneliness in the teaching of our Torah, yet the act of study and the journey of discovery are dangerous. The more we learn, the more we seek to know and the more we find that knowledge is elusive. I've always understood Torah to be akin to the letters of a lover who lives far away. The items bring us closer to him or her, but they also remind us of the distance. Each word of our lover's letter takes on cosmic importance, because it is our only record of their presence. The Torah, like the letter, is a snapshot of reality. Its words are finite and it is frozen in time. Its presence reminds us what we are missing and how far we stand from entering the palace.

As painful as it is to stand outside of the castle, however, we have company. Everyone who has ever sought truth stands beside us, from Moses to Rabbi Akiva, from our rabbis to our students. We all gaze into the window together, hoping for a glimpse. We are a community of voyeurs, forged by the commonality of our yearning for what is inside.

Israel, the Persecuted People

Part of the reason it is so painful when we feel God has left us is that we have no other source of comfort. True, the Jewish people have each other. But sometimes when we as a people suffer, we need another to help us. And all too often, it feels as if we are a people alone.

Ever since Abraham first ventured into Egypt during one of the many famines that ravaged ancient Israel, our ancestors have felt like pariahs among the other nations of the world. Even in those first moments of Jewish peoplehood, Abraham does not belong. Fearing that the Pharaoh will kill him and take his wife Sarah, he pretends she is his sister. He hides his true identity, knowing that if he proudly shows off his family and his heritage, it will mean his destruction (Genesis 12:10–20).

The clash Abraham experiences, between being true to his people and hiding a piece of himself to survive, has been one of the fundamental tensions of living as a Jew in the world. Yes, there is so much to celebrate about being Jewish. There is deep wisdom in our tradition, powerful ritual, and enduring communal bonds. But when times get tough for the Jewish people, the foundational choice of the Jew is between guilt and shame.

Abraham chose guilt. He knew it would be challenging to be fully himself in Egypt, so he hid a part of his identity. So afraid to publicly proclaim his love for Sarah, he was forced to conceal it. Walking into Egypt, Abraham was denied the ability to say, "This is my wife, these are my people, and this my heritage." The Rabbis were so uncomfortable with Abraham's secrecy that they created a story to defend him. They imagined that as he entered Egypt, he hid Sarah in a box (*Genesis Rabbah* 45:5). Away from view, she could sneak into Egypt unharmed. When the customs agent cross-examined him about its content, however, he was forced to reveal her. Only when discovered did he then panic and deny their relationship.

Yet, even this apologetic story does little to change the reality of Abraham's actions. After letting her go, Abraham is left to wonder if he made the right decision. His wife is in the royal palace, his future uncertain. In denying his wife, Abraham made the choice that countless Jews have been forced to make throughout the generations; he chose his safety over his people. Whether speaking about forced conversions in medieval Spain, Jewish children raised in convents during the Holocaust, or immigrants who changed their names on coming to America, this choice has been part of the fabric of the Jewish people since its inception. While sometimes necessary, choosing life over faith, preservation over heritage, comes with its costs. Little can relieve the internal guilt left after the decision. The experience of persecution is a lonely one because if you leave, there is nowhere to turn for support. You won't find comfort among your persecutors—Abraham couldn't seek aid from the Egyptians just as Spanish Marranos couldn't find understanding in their Christian neighbors. Conversely, you also can't turn back. Denying your heritage is one of the cardinal sins of the Jewish people.[1] For this reason, history has judged his actions. Nachmanides wrote in the Middle Ages that because of Abraham's decision to leave Israel, which led to his lie, the people were condemned in future generations to live in exile in the land of Egypt.[2]

Yet, if Abraham and others like him stay Jewish, the alternative is no better. Rather than guilt, the Jewish people are forced to confront shame. Our tradition has countless examples of the torment of living as a Jew in a world of persecution. The psalmist writes, "I lie awake; I am like a lone bird upon a roof. All day long my enemies revile me; my deriders use my name to curse" (Psalm 102:8–9). Sadly, this derision lasted through the ages. It was present after the destruction of the First Temple, when in exile, sitting by the rivers of Babylon, our captors taunted us by making us sing songs from Jerusalem (Psalm 137:3). It existed in ancient Rome. Our Rabbis tell the story of the nations of the world sitting in theaters and circuses mocking the Jews. In jest, they dress their camels up in Jewish garb and bring in mimes with shaved heads, comparing the actors' poor appearances to Jews on Friday night (*Lamentations Rabbah*, proem 17). Eventually this attitude made its way to modern day. One of most indelible sets of images from the Holocaust are the pictures of prominent rabbis up in many museums who were forced to shave their beards or dance atop Torah scrolls to the tune of Nazi laughter and mirth. It seems our Rabbis were correct when they said that the Jewish people "could not remain in tranquility for even six hours" (*Exodus Rabbah* 41:7).

The choice between guilt and shame is surely a lonely one. Either alternative comes with an unhealthy dose of suffering. Two thousand years ago, Rabbi Akiva articulated this choice. Asked by Pappus ben Judah why he continued to teach Torah in the face of persecutions, Akiva responded with a parable:

> A fox was once walking alongside of a river, and he saw fish going in swarms from one place to another. He said to them: From what are you fleeing? They replied: From the nets cast for us by men. He said to them: Would you like to come up on to the dry land so that you and I can live together in the way that my ancestors lived with your ancestors? They replied: Aren't you the one that they call the cleverest of animals? You are not clever but foolish. If we are afraid in the element in

which we live, how much more in the element in which
we would die! (Talmud, *Berachot* 61b)

The historical choice for the Jewish people is impossible: live in danger
as a Jew or let your heritage die. Yet the former choice, while isolating, comes with tremendous benefit. Coupled with shame is the story
of Jewish perseverance. In our loneliness, we show the generations to
come that they do not suffer alone. Every generation deals with the
pain of feeling as if they are the last generation of Jews and that their
suffering may finally get the best of them, a phenomenon that the
early twentieth-century Jewish philosopher Simon Rawidowicz once
described as "ever-dying" in his essay "Israel: The Ever-Dying People."
Yet, that pain, that alienation, is not in vain. Our "ever-dying" status is
redemptive. Rawidowicz observes, "Our incessant dying means unin-
terrupted living, rising, standing up, beginning anew."[3]

Our loneliness yields strength. Our isolation forges courage. The
pain of having no one on whom to rely means we must turn inward for
support. Our greatest institutions, our most insightful texts, our most
thoughtful art have all been created at times when we felt all hope was
lost. Time has made it hard to be a Jew, but our people have helped one
another to transcend. Together we laugh in the face of history.

Jerusalem: A Lonely City for a Lonely People

If individuals, peoples, and even God can feel lonely, it comes as no
surprise that there are places in which loneliness pervades. Jerusalem
has seen so much sorrow. Pain haunts the city like a ghost. Its air is
saturated with suffering.

Our Rabbis often personified nature. They imagined that animals
and trees yearn for companionship just as we do (*Lamentations Rabbah*
1:30). Even time seeks a mate; Shabbat was said to suffer when she realized that as the seventh day, all the other days of the week had already
paired up (*Genesis Rabbah* 11:8). However, there is a special place in our
tradition for the loneliness of Jerusalem.

Isaiah once spoke of the city as "homesteads deserted, forsaken like
a wilderness" (Isaiah 27:10). Jeremiah said:

> Lonely sits the city
> Once great with people!
> She that was great among nations
> Is become like a widow;
> The princess among states
> Is become a thrall.
>
> (LAMENTATIONS 1:1)

Even the roads to Jerusalem mourn. Where once pilgrims trod their paths, now they too mourn, empty and destroyed (*Lamentations Rabbah* 1:30).

It is no coincidence that a lonely people found the loneliest of places to build their Temple. We don't like dissonance. It's a strange feeling when your inner world does not match the outer one. Whether we realize it or not, we know this tension. We often have an unsettled feeling when a funeral falls on a beautiful day. When we ache, we want even the wind to know our pain. Jerusalem is the land of pathos. It understands us. Its walls cry out beside us.

Because it is so in tune to the inner world of the Jewish people, we know that when Jerusalem will rejoice, it will mean an end to our pain as well. Our prayers stand with Jerusalem, and we pray as Isaiah did that "never again shall be heard there the sounds of weeping and wailing" (Isaiah 65:19). We hope that when our crying ends we will warrant a better era, when the prophet Zechariah's vision is realized and "the squares of the city shall be crowded with boys and girls playing in the squares" (Zechariah 8:5). If Jerusalem, which means "the city of peace," finds tranquility and joy, there is hope. When we lack the strength to seek healing for our own brokenness, Jerusalem gives us an alternative place for our prayers. A mirror to our suffering, we watch and pray anxiously for its healing, knowing that if it can find wholeness, so too can we.

The Power of Parable

Throughout this book we have looked at a diversity of personalities, all of whom have dealt with deep loneliness in their own way. Ranging from Moses to Jeremiah, Hannah to David, God to the Jewish people, these character studies have aimed to show the pervasiveness of loneliness throughout our canon and its enduring import on our individual and communal story. Throughout these pages, we have attempted to show that the Bible provides a model for those who seek a companion in their pain. The reason the Bible works is because at its core it is seen best as parable. Writing about the power of parable, Israeli scholar Micah Goodman explains:

> Although many of the biblical stories did not actually take place in reality, they are still true—because the lessons that emerge from their parables are true. If an event is historical, then it is something that happened in the past; if it is a parable, then it is a story that also "happens" in the present and the future. Turning story into allegory ... strengthens its meaning and transforms it from an isolated event into a universal truth.[4]

Our ancestors' suffering did not happen once. All mourners contain a piece of Isaac's suffering. Jeremiah and David are a part of all those leaders who feel alienation. Tamar's uneasiness at finding love is the same uneasiness many of us feel. Those who are sick feel much of Uzziah's alienation. Our sacred writings whisper lessons on loneliness through parables of pain. If parables teach us that the events of another's life are not isolated, that means ours are not either. We may feel alone, but our experiences are universal. Story is our all-pervasive companion.

PART 3

Coping with Loneliness in Ourselves and Others

7

From the Depths

Learning to Cry Out

There is a story told of Rabbi Yochanan, who became ill (Talmud, *Berachot* 5b). Upon learning of his friend's plight, Rabbi Chanina came to visit him. Looking at his friend's suffering, Chanina asked Yochanan a simple question, "Are these afflictions dear to you?" While answering in the affirmative might have made him look weak and unfaithful, Yochanan put his pride aside and responded, yes. He did not appreciate his suffering. "Neither they [his afflictions] nor their reward," he proclaimed.

In one simple statement, Yochanan showed a tremendous amount of bravery. He spoke against God and against his sickness. By being honest, he sought connection to Chanina. He told his truth and cried out in his pain. His sickness was not fair in his eyes, and he wanted a remedy. Consequently, Chanina responded, "Give me your hand," as he reached toward his companion. Rabbi Yochanan gave him his hand, and Rabbi Chanina revived him.

Reflecting back on this story, the author of our Talmud asks an important question: Why did Yochanan need Chanina's help? He was just as powerful and gifted as his colleague. Couldn't he have helped himself? The Talmud answers its own question with a power teaching: "A captive cannot release himself from prison."

When we are trapped by our illnesses, by our isolation, and by our loneliness, even the strongest of us need another to come by to free us from our captivity. Locked behind the gate of despair, only another has the power to deliver us and absolve us of our pain. The story of Yochanan teaches an important lesson: if we are truly to help ourselves combat loneliness, we need to learn to call out to another, for only when we get the courage to open our lips and let our mouths declare our sufferings can we hope that someone may notice and begin to take steps to help us to heal.

Letting Yourself Feel Sadness

Before we can seek out another, we need to learn to acknowledge our own pain. Yet, too many of us, out of the fear of feeling vulnerable or weak, push normal levels of sadness down and fail to see its power. We emphasize joy above all, taking the commandment in the Torah to feel "nothing but happiness" literally (Deuteronomy 16:15). However, rather than allowing joy and sadness to commingle among us, each with an established seat at the emotional table, we silence sadness. We lock it away, not realizing that if you push an emotion down, it will find its way back to you eventually.

Two summers ago, society got a gift in the form of Disney's *Inside Out*. The premise of the movie is that five dominant and personified emotions govern the brain of Riley, a young adolescent girl. They are Anger, Fear, Disgust, Joy, and Sadness. Of the five emotions, Joy is the leader. Joy makes Riley successful. Joy helps her connect with others and be productive in school. All the other emotions are ancillary, including Sadness, a somewhat pathetic character voiced by Phyllis Smith.

As Riley ages, however, Sadness begins to emerge as a major force in her personality. At first Joy resists this. She does what many of us have done before. She draws a circle on the floor and places Sadness inside. "This is your circle of Sadness," she seems to say. "You can be inside here, but don't come out further than that."

But eventually she learns to appreciate Sadness. In one profound scene, we learn why. The movie is filled with a number of minor characters, one of whom is an imaginary friend that Riley no longer believes in. At one point, this imaginary friend has an opportunity to save Joy and Sadness but is crippled by regret about his past. While Joy tries everything to cheer him up, her actions have no effect. Only when Sadness sits down next to him and agrees that his situation is in fact tragic, only when she shows him that she understands his sadness as well, does he open up and eventually have a catharsis of tears. Here Sadness has done something that Joy cannot. Sadness has become the avenue to connection between two yearning souls.

However, we are often so scared of our own sadness that we keep it bottled up. We don't realize that living a life with a full emotional range must include a substantial helping of sorrow. And without acknowledging our own pain, we certainly can't reach out to others and search for authentic connection when we hurt.

Classically, a person is not supposed to be a prayer leader of a congregation until he or she has reached the age of thirty. Though many reasons have been given for this strange law, the most cited answer is that in order to be a good prayer leader, one must have experienced a few episodes of brokenheartedness. How else can we trust that our leader can understand the burdens of our community, empathize with our struggles, and advocate on our behalf? The psalmist tells us that "God is close to the brokenhearted; those crushed in spirit God delivers" (Psalm 34:19). Those who have lived long enough to fully experience sadness have the well-worn soul to carry their community's pain on their shoulders as they communicate with God. As our Talmud teaches, "Every gate to heaven may be locked except for the gates of tears" (*Bava Metzia* 59a).

Sharing in sadness is so important for personal growth and communal cohesion that our tradition creates space for these moments throughout our calendar. We break a glass at the end of a wedding, our most joyous time, to remember and mourn the destruction of the Holy Temple. After losing a loved one, Jewish law forces a person to pause for seven days, a process known as shivah, to sit with their pain and receive it.

Perhaps the greatest reminder not to fear sadness comes during our shofar service on Rosh Hashanah. Our ancestors loved to imagine metaphors for the sounding of the shofar. For some, it was meant to be a war horn; for others, an alarm clock for the soul. For Maimonides, however, the shofar was meant to sound like crying. As we know, there are many types of tears. The long blast known as *t'kiah* is meant to remind us of the sound of someone moaning. The three shortened blasts of *sh'varim* are meant to remind us of the deep sobbing of someone who is heavily burdened. *T'ruah*, nine very quick bursts in rapid succession, are meant to sound like intense wailing.[1]

Each Rosh Hashanah, our shofar reminds us of one simple message: sadness is a constant in our lives and in the lives of everyone we know. We cannot avoid it. It sometimes saturates the air. But just as we aren't afraid to let the shofar sound, we also shouldn't fear un-bottling our sadness. For, even though the shofar is an external manifestation of our inner pain, there is something uplifting about hearing its cry.

That is because sadness rarely travels alone. When we greet sadness and allow ourselves the space to feel it, we are often met soon after with a substantial helping of strength, courage, insight, and even joy. As a rabbi, I've seen many in my community experience the positive effects of sadness. I've watched mourners, so sad they could barely talk at their shivah, allow that pain in and eventually heal. I've watched those struggling with job loss vent about the silence they receive when contacting employers and, after this catharsis, find the strength to completely overhaul their resume. I've heard parents bemoan how difficult child rearing is and, once they feel heard, muster the strength to address this or that issue with their kids.

Sadness works because our souls are anti-fragile, a term coined by the economist Nassim Nicholas Taleb.[2] Something that is fragile breaks when put under pressure. However, something that is anti-fragile gets stronger. We build muscle by first creating small tears in the tissue, and we strengthen our bones by first breaking them down. Societal movements, like revolutions, need efforts to quash them to coalesce. And like these examples, our souls become richer and deeper if they encounter sadness.

Yet, too often we distract ourselves to avoid allowing sadness in. We busy ourselves with our devices or we tell ourselves stories about why we shouldn't be upset. But instead of saving ourselves, we just train our souls to engage with the world on a safe, but surface level. We may not be truly sad, but by muting our emotional register, we keep our-selves also from being profoundly happy. The effort it takes to silence one emotion will blunt our ability to feel all emotions.

Our Rabbis articulated a similar notion. There is a teaching in our tradition that when God created each day, he called it *tov*, "good." How-ever, when God created the sixth day, the day when humanity appeared, God called it *tov m'od*, "very good." Reflecting back on what was so impor-tant about that day, our Rabbis came up with a number of interpretations, but one has always struck me. They teach that it was "good" that through humans the world would have more joy. But it was "very good," for all the reasons we have considered, that through humanity the world would have a mixture of joy and sadness (*Genesis Rabbah* 9:8).

We have the power to confront our loneliness and find healing in our sorrow. But we can't move forward until we acknowledge our pain. To open ourselves up to others, we have to look deeply into our souls even if we fear what we might find. Embracing sadness is the only way we can find ourselves ready to call out for help.

The Power of Speaking the Truth

Anyone familiar with psychotherapy knows that there is incredible power in speaking one's truth. Speech is transformative. Yet, we tend to bottle up our emotions. Afraid to let them out, our anger, loneliness, and despair well up. With nowhere to go, our inner life can consume us. But speaking these emotions means that they do not control us. We can free ourselves of our burdens, but we must first articulate them in order to move past them.

If the Torah's account of creation teaches us anything, it is that words were God's tool to create the world. Had God not spoken, "Let there be light" (Genesis 1:3), it would not have existed. We stand in a universe that was created by speech. And like God, we too can use our words to create worlds. Without verbalizing our truths, our lives would be "formless and empty" (Genesis 1:2, translation mine). Bringing our pain to the surface is the first step in banishing it from our midst.

Our Rabbis taught, "Words that are in the heart are not words" (Talmud, *Kiddushin* 49b). Our tradition understands how wrong we can be when we make assumptions about another. When we guess what words remain in the heart, we are often wrong. And though our sages made this statement in the context of assuming intent during a business deal, their adage rings true when trying to assess another's emotional life. Our desires, our yearnings, and our pain cannot be fully realized until we express them.

Rebbe Nachman has an apt teaching that speaks to the power of words. In his seminal work *Likutei Moharan*, Nachman explains that when one sins, his sin is engraved on his bones. Etched deep within his core, he carries his sin around with him wherever he goes. However, the sinner may rid himself of this stain if he opens his mouth in "spoken confession." Only through speaking does he erase the sin from his bones and build for himself a "kingdom of holiness."[3]

Although Nachman here is talking about sin, his teaching applies to one who is in pain as well. We carry with us the scars of the past. We fear embracing meaningful relationships because of past slights. We are angry at a small group, but we direct that anger toward all people. We engender grudges and fuel vendettas, unable to forgive. And the deeper these emotional injuries run, the more removed we become from those who can cure us of our loneliness. Our alienation becomes etched onto our bones. We are unable to erase it. Yet, if we follow Nachman's advice, if we speak our truths and our pains, we can take steps to rid ourselves of them.

Our sages understood just how easy it is to hide inside of ourselves. They liken the creation of humanity to the building of a city with underground chambers, passages, and caves (*Genesis Rabbah* 24:1). Although, our Rabbis understood that God, who was the architect of this city, can easily find us when we hide within the crevices of these structures, they acknowledge that others cannot. To be human is to be created with a complex inner life that others cannot access. Perhaps this is the reason that the blessing we recite when we see a large group of Jews is "Blessed are You, God ... the Knower of Secrets" (Talmud, *Berachot* 58a). No one but God has the capacity to see deep within us and know what we hide from others. If we are to let others know of our inner life, we have to let it out.

Perhaps the greatest driver of loneliness in our lives is shame. Though often mistaken for guilt, shame is much more insidious. Whereas guilt is the regret over an action, shame is regret for the self. A guilty person says, "I did wrong." Shame causes us to say, "I am wrong." While guilt encourages us to reach out to others to right a misdeed, shame forces us inward, afraid that others will judge us if they knew our truth.[4]

Shame cannot exist without its counterpart, secrecy. Secrecy by its very definition keeps our innermost thoughts bottled up. Since our nightmares are almost always worse than reality, the only way to deal with our shame is to face it. However, we are often so afraid that others will judge us for our shortcomings that we keep our true selves hidden. Shame is a poison. It eats away at our soul and degrades our spirit. Whereas hiding our shame gives it time to continue to wreak havoc, speaking it releases it, taking away its power.

Yet, despite its role in alleviating shame, we are all too often given the erroneous message that only trouble will come from truth-telling. There is a tragic moment in the Bible when David's son Amnon forces himself on his sister Tamar and rapes her. After the episode, Tamar confides in another of her brothers, Absalom, and tells him of the assault. Rather than support his sister or try to comfort her, Absalom admonishes her, telling her not to let the violation upset her and then warning her to keep it secret. Though Absalom was trying to protect her and his family, his reaction was disastrous for his sister. The Bible tells us that from that conversation forward, "Tamar lived desolate in Absalom's house" (2 Samuel 13:20, translation mine). Here, the Bible's use of the word "desolate" (*shomemah*) is no accident. Like the barren deserts that are usually described with this word,[5] Tamar's secret cut her off from civilization. So afraid of being found out, Tamar was doomed to a hermetic life. Secrecy would keep the shame of her rape forever present in her life. Loneliness is found most acutely among the secrets we cannot share.

If her brother had acted differently and encouraged her to speak about the rape (when ready), Tamar would have found a way out of that prison. Two thousand years ago, two rabbis, Ammi and Assi, engaged in a debate about the merits of speech (Talmud, *Sanhedrin* 100b). When faced with anxiety, when haunted by the inner demons that keep us apart from others, how should we act? Assi responded that we should "banish it from our minds." Ammi disagreed. To battle our shame, doubt, alienation, and loneliness, he said, we should "speak about it to others."

History and psychology have shown that that Ammi is right. His warning that we cannot banish our loneliness on our own is echoed in one of my favorite Hasidic proverbs. In it a group of disciples approach their rabbi and ask him what they can do about the darkness and evil in the world. He suggests that they take brooms into the basement and sweep away the darkness. However, when they try, nothing happens. They return and he tells them to try shouting at the darkness, but the darkness remains. They then try to beat the darkness with sticks, but it goes nowhere. Finally, he suggests that they light a candle, and the darkness disappears.

Our darkness cannot be swept away, shouted away, or beaten away. We too need lights. Speaking our pain opens others up to be lights of compassion, love, and openness. True, not everyone will give us messages of safety and assurance. Tamar learned this lesson the hard way from her brother's callous response. Yet, we all have someone in our lives, be it friends, family, teachers, mentors, neighbors, or rabbis, whom we can turn to in our time of need. They will do for our darkness what a million sticks and brooms cannot. If we open ourselves to their love, if we voice our pain, if we seek their support, our shame stands no chance, and our loneliness loses its chief vehicle.

The Importance of Crying Out

One of the great mysteries of Jewish history is why God decided to redeem the Jewish people from Egypt when God did. Over the generations, commentators have given their interpretations, but my favorite answer surrounds the idea that God was ready to redeem them from bondage only when they were ready to ask for divine help.

Over the generations, the Jewish people in Egypt became complacent. Rabbi Hanoch of Alexander once wrote, "The real exile of Egypt was that they learned to endure it." They acquiesced to the hand of their Egyptian taskmasters for years. They lived among brutality, unable to see a brighter future for themselves. However, slavery became too much for them. Our Rabbis tell us that Pharaoh got sick and his magicians told him the only cure for his ailment was Jewish blood (*Exodus Rabbah* 1:34). Eventually, faced with wanton death and threatened lives, they cried out to God, and hearing this, God made the decision to save them.

We must imagine that this was not the first time the people cried out. Every lash of the taskmaster's whip, every angry insult, every callous command must have produced a sound. However, the cry that reached God was unique. Our Rabbis teach that this cry was not one of complaint or regret; it was a fully throated emotional gasp, the last act of a people who had reached their breaking point. There are two ways to cry out. We can call out from an intellectual place—"It's not fair! Why me?"—or from a seat of emotion—"I hurt. I am wounded." It is this second cry, say our Rabbis, our primordial animal release, often too powerful for words, that moved God and will move all those that hear us.

The *Zohar* has a powerful statement by Rabbi Judah about this kind of cry:

> Of all the three expressions for prayer used in the Exodus narrative, crying out (*tsa'akah*) is the greatest of all because it is entirely a matter of the heart ... this crying comes nearer to the Holy One blessed be He than imploring and praying in words. Rabbi Berachiah said: When people pray and weep and cry so intensely that they are unable to find words to express their sorrow, theirs is the perfect prayer, for it is in their heart, and this will never return to them empty.[6]

However, when we suffer, many of us avoid letting others see this side of us. We worry that this show of naked emotion will make us feel exposed. We fear looking weak. We doubt others will accept such a display with openness and love, so we hold back.

We might even speak our pain to others, telling them about our isolation, unpacking our alienation, sharing the intellectual struggles of our loneliness. But that's not enough. When we feel alone, we need the emotional presence of others. If we engage them on an intellectual level, we will receive comfort of the mind. But if we put our broken hearts on display, we will speak to a different, more primitive, part of them.

The great Hasidic rabbi Elimelech of Lizhensk used to write about the powerful mystical notion that what we feel on earth can literally "light up" those parts of God in heaven.[7] When we act, we flip a cosmic switch above. Our compassion turns on God's compassion. Our mercy bolsters God's mercy. It's as if each of these attributes lies dormant until we remind God they exist.

So too, much of our emotional lives remains hidden. We have the power to be compassionate, loving, and nurturing. We have the courage and the presence. But we often need a jolt to remember these virtues. When those who are lonely cry out to us, their plea can rouse us from our stupor. Their strength reminds us to be strong; their openness commands us to be open. But without that first cry, without that honest call, we may never wake up to their reality. We need their plea to "light up" our virtues. Only then can we open our arms and our hearts to them and begin to address their pain.

Learning to Trust Others

It's not easy to trust that when we call, another will answer. Being raw before another is a frightening prospect. If we reach out to loved ones and they do not answer, their silence only reinforces our invisibility and isolation. But in spite of the risks, we need to trust others. We need to believe that when we call, we will hear an answer.

The people who love and care about us want to help us grow. Love, by its nature, means wishing a better tomorrow for another. No one who truly loves us can remain silent when we call out. They will respond, usually providing more of what we need than we have asked for. Their desire will pour forth and they will be compelled to answer. Hearing your pain, they will live out the dictum of Rav Kook, "I speak not because I have the power to speak; I speak because I don't have the power to remain silent."[8] Whether we trust them enough to open the door to their love by crying out will mean the difference between their hearing us or their remaining oblivious to our suffering.

There is a story in the Talmud about Rabbi Akiva, who was asked during a time of Roman persecutions by Rabbi Shimon bar Yochai to teach him Torah. Knowing that the government had outlawed Torah study and that by teaching it, both he and his students would lose their lives, Akiva refused. Akiva was reluctant to open himself up to the dangers of taking a student. But Shimon bar Yochai would not be dissuaded. He looked at his teacher and spoke words of incredible depth and truth: "The cow wants to nurse more than the calf wants to suckle" (*Pesachim* 112a). In one simple phrase, Rabbi Shimon summarized not only the desire of the teacher but also the passion of all of those who feel love for another and wish to be useful in their time of need. Our desire to help usually supersedes another's desire for our aid.

When we love something, we want to give it gifts. I have had so many congregants who love our synagogue ask me how they might give back. They are looking for an opportunity to volunteer their time and energy so they might repay, in part, what they have gained from us. The love of people works the same way. I get so much from my parents and siblings, my coworkers and my friends. I often feel that there is nothing I can do to tangibly convey my connection and show my gratitude. When others ask me for help, they provide me an occasion to endow them with my love and I am thankful for the opportunity to repay their goodness

Our tradition's famous maxim to "judge others favorably" (*Mishnah Avot* 1:6) literally means in Hebrew to tilt the scales intentionally toward the side of merit. We all have a choice. We can see others as unsympathetic and threatening, or in spite of all our fears, we can tip the balance toward trust. We can see others for the kind, open people we hope they are and take a risk with our hearts. It's the only path out of loneliness, and if we follow it, we might be surprised how quickly others accompany us on our trek.

Learning to Help Yourself

It once happened that Chanina ben Dosa saw a group of people from his city bringing offerings up to Jerusalem (*Ecclesiastes Rabbah* 1:1). Wanting to bring something himself, he entered a wasteland and found a precious stone buried in a rock face. He chiseled it and polished it, excited to bring it as an offering. However, the stone was too heavy to carry. He found workers, but their fee was too much. A group of angels heard of his plight and came down to help him. "We can carry it for you," they said, "but you will have to place a hand and finger on it along with us." Chanina ben Dosa agreed, and the minute he touched the stone, he found himself magically transported to Jerusalem.

The lesson of this story is clear. We can't rely on others for everything. If we are to move the heavy stones of our lives, if we are to deal with loneliness, to cope with isolation, we need to help others to help us. Even the smallest step forward on our part can do a world of good and can mean the difference between being stuck or being transported. Whether we have the courage to call out, whether we can speak our truth, whether we can transcend our shame, these all determine our success.

When we are lonely, we feel we are far from others. But we can bridge that chasm. Be like the boy, says our tradition, who is far away from his father. When he is told to return home, he does not have the strength to make the full journey. Soon he receives a letter, "Come as far as you can, and I will take care of the rest" (based on *Pesikta Rabbati* 44:9). Though our Rabbis wrote this story to explain how to transcend our isolation from God, their words hold equally true when explaining how to re-engage with those we love. We have to take the first steps. We cannot expect help unless we give of ourselves. And then, after taking that risk, we have to trust that when we fall, others will be there to carry us forward toward home.

8

Hearing the Call

When Another Cries Out

One of the most overlooked characters of compassion in the Bible is in fact one of the most controversial. Known as the Witch of En-dor, she appears briefly in the book of Samuel and disappears soon after (1 Samuel 28). Though she would spark a millennia-long debate about the place of witchcraft and necromancy in our tradition, few of our classical commentators acknowledge her incredible humanity and love.

We first meet the Witch of En-dor on the eve of a great battle between the Israelites and the Philistine armies. Saul, who at the time is king of Israel, fears he might lose the battle. Though he seeks God's guidance, he is met with silence. At the behest of his servants, Saul seeks out the Witch of En-dor for advice and guidance. We know little about Saul's mind-set as he approaches her abode, but our ancient Rabbis tell us that a darkness was upon Saul's soul as he drew near, so that even though he and his men visited her by day, "it seemed to them dark as night."[1]

Soon the witch conjures up the dead soul of the prophet Samuel. Samuel is upset that he has been disturbed from his eternal slumber and angrily relays the truth to Saul: he is finished as king. His army will be defeated, he and his sons will die, and David, his younger adversary, will assume the throne. Utterly bewildered, Saul falls on his face, fully lacking strength.

Yet, no sooner does Saul lament his fate than the Witch of En-dor steps forward to help him. The Bible tells us explicitly she saw how "greatly disturbed he was" (1 Samuel 28:21). Quickly, she responds to him. The witch goes up to Saul, who is now sitting on the ground. She tells him that she has heard him and reminds him of the risk she undertook in helping him. Then, she implores him to take a similar risk, implying, "Permit me to help you." Knowing that Saul would not accept her help or comfort she starts small: "Let me set before you a bit of food. Eat, and then you will have the strength to go on your way" (1 Samuel 28:22). At first, Saul refuses her kindness, but after his servants press him further, he acquiesces.[2] The witch goes out, slaughters a calf, and bakes him unleavened cakes. Hours later, when she is done cooking and when Saul has processed and integrated the news, she brings Saul the food.[3] With compassion and love, she serves him dinner, granting him leave when he is ready.

Commenting on this story in his book on King David, Rabbi David Wolpe quotes Israeli scholar Moshe Halbertal, who "once remarked that he considered the Witch of En-Dor the most altruistic character in the entire chronicle and her act of nourishing the condemned king a highpoint of kindness."[4]

Just as the Jewish tradition is filled with the stories of those suffering from loneliness, it too contains characters like the Witch of En-dor, whose compassion and openness overflow the narrative and inspire us to do more for those suffering in our midst. This chapter will discuss a few of the lessons that the Witch of En-dor knew innately that made her such a comfort to Saul, as well as a few that are not present in the story but are important tools for all of us. Though many of her virtues were innate to her character, we can cultivate them within us. Doing so, we might better answer when another cries out.

Do No Harm: What Not to Say

Perhaps the most important part of the Witch of En-dor's response is what is not said. At no point does she blame Saul for his downfall. She makes no excuses, finds no fault, and conjectures no reason for his predicament. When we see another suffering, the first step is to examine how our words may serve as a stumbling block to healing; just as our sentiment can build worlds, so too can our insensitivity destroy them.

Perhaps the most famous counterexample to the Witch of Endor's careful words appears in the clumsy comfort given to Job by his friends. The book of Job tells the story of a righteous individual who gets caught up in a bet between God and his advisor HaSatan.[5] To prove that Job can handle anything and still remain faithful, God gives HaSatan permission to take Job's house, wealth, and children from him. At first Job remains faithful, but soon his suffering becomes too great. His body betrays him, and suffering from boils, he breaks down. Seeing him wallow, his wife implores him to curse God and die. Although Job doesn't choose death, he does call out in his suffering, "Perish the day on which I was born, and the night it was announced, 'A male has been conceived!'" (Job 3:3).

Soon after, Job is visited by a group of friends, Eliphaz the Temanite, Bildad the Shuhite, and Zophar the Naamathite. Their job is "to go and console and comfort him" (Job 2:11). Yet, they fall short in their task. Instead of bringing Job comfort, they blame Job for his suffering, defending God's actions and God's providence. Time and again, Job defends himself, claiming he has done nothing to deserve his plight. Each time he cries out, however, his call falls on deaf ears. His friends are so busy being pious that they fail to be compassionate.

Reading Job's story many generations later, our ancient Rabbis criticized the visitors' actions. Examining their words closely, they label the friend's false comfort *ona'at d'varim*, literally "wronging through words" (Talmud, *Bava Metzia* 58b). *Ona'at d'varim* takes many forms. We commit it when we ask a shopkeeper for the price of an item we do not intend to buy or when we remind penitents of their corrupt past.

Though these examples seem disparate, they are not. All deal with words that overreach and distort. They are a kind of fraud. We misrepresent ourselves when we seek an item we will not buy, and we devalue the present state of the righteous when we invoke their past. In the case of Job's comforters, they belittle the complexities of life with easy answers and victim blaming.

According to the Rabbis, the worst line uttered to Job, and the emblematic example of *ona'at d'varim*, comes from Job 4:6–7, "Is not your piety your confidence, your integrity your hope? Think now, what innocent man ever perished?" This is a sentiment that we all too often express to those who are suffering, amounting in essence to the statement "If you were really such a righteous person you wouldn't be suffering. You must not fear God enough. If you were as pious as you claim, you would be confident and hopeful that the future would turn out right." There is a range of acceptable answers we may give when another is suffering, but this is not one of them. To blame the victim and to declare that God is enacting punishment for their previous deeds is certainly outside the scope of our certainty. We don't know the mysteries of the universe. Eliphaz, the speaker of this quote, is overreaching and, worse, possibly misrepresenting God, who never asked for his defense in the first place.

Though the book of Job serves as a warning to avoid senseless posturing, people frequently ignore its wisdom and overreach with words when another is suffering. When we are faced with others who are in pain, we can't help but try to comfort them. Yet, all too often, our comforting words are not actually directed to the sufferer, but aimed toward ourselves. We try to offer support but our aid gets muddled as we reassure ourselves that the world is indeed just and try to talk ourselves out of our religious doubts. It's hard to watch another in pain. It reminds us of our frailty. So, without realizing it, we speak the words *we* need to hear, rather than the words they do.

Many adults know what phrases to avoid. Our loved ones may not be "in a better place." Your suffering may not exist "for a reason." God may not be "following a plan." Yet, just because a statement is not tactless doesn't mean it is helpful. Any answer, even one that brings good tidings, has the potential to overreach. And this is especially true for those who are suffering from loneliness.

I once had a conversation with a congregant who had recently broken up with her boyfriend. Though it was only a short relationship—about six months—it was her longest in many years. She had been out on countless dates and tried nearly every dating site, but she was not finding anyone. By all accounts, she should not have had a problem dating. She was pretty, sociable, intelligent, and funny. She had a great group of friends and was successful in every part of her life except finding love. When I encountered her, she had just had an argument with her mother, who, trying to be helpful, had said, "Just keep looking; he's out there."

The reason she was upset was not because she felt like her mother was out of line, but because her mother was overreaching. "How does she know?" she asked me. "Maybe I won't!" I realized in that moment that what she needed to hear from her mother was not encouragement that she would find love, but reassurance that her life would be okay if she didn't. Her mother was making a classic mistake we all make when facing those who are lonely: she addressed her problem, not her person.

The Witch of En-dor does none of this. When she sees Saul suffering, she does not conjecture a reason. Her words are simple and supportive. Her actions teach us to speak from a wellspring of support, not a fountain of knowledge. "There is a time for everything," reminds King Solomon (Ecclesiastes 3:1). In our lives, there is a time to ask the big questions; we are on a sacred mission to wrestle with profound truths and make meaning from our experiences. But in the face of suffering, fishing for reasons does more harm than good. When someone is lonely, they don't need our thoughts; they need our love.

Non-Judgment: Accepting Another's Truth

When Saul was suffering, the Witch of En-dor gave him a gift: the space to grieve in his own way. She knew that all suffering is subjective and accepted it fully. When others say they are lonely, it does little good to judge the validity or veracity of their claim. Instead, our job is to allow their experience to stand, providing a platform for authentic and unmitigated sentiment.

No one can judge another's pain. Even the seemingly smallest setbacks have the possibility to cause anguish to another. "To what extent does suffering go?" ask our Rabbis. "Even if one reaches into a pocket to remove three coins and comes up with two" (Talmud, *Arachin* 16a). We have all seen others cry at something we consider insignificant. We silently judge their right to tears, knowing that we have reserved ours for grievances much greater. Yet, their pain is sincere, their distress is true. Acknowledging the authenticity of their response is the first step to securing the authenticity of ours. True comfort can only come from true acceptance.

The corollary to this teaching is that the reverse is also true; just because we assume someone should suffer doesn't mean they will. There is a story in our Midrash about Rabbi Meir, who went to console his neighbor Abinimos Gadera after the death of his mother (*Ruth Rabbah* 2:13). Walking into the house, he saw Abinimos in mourning. As a good friend would, he sat with him and helped him through his travail. Some time later, he got the news that Abinimos had lost his father. As he did before, Meir went to his friend, but this time when he walked in, he noticed Abinimos was engaged in normal occupations. At first he was surprised; why was Abinimos not profoundly affected by his father's death? Hadn't he just faced a major loss? Soon Meir realized that Abinimos had a different relationship with his father than with his mother. Facing a different kind of pain, he did not need Meir's comfort in the same way. Like a good friend, Meir avoided judgment. He followed his friend's lead.

Part of the reason we shouldn't claim to know another's pain is that each of us is a moving target. We are constantly changing. We grow apart from friends who are not the same people we knew decades earlier. Our parents soften or harden with age. I've talked to many older couples who have told me that though they were married for fifty years, over the course of that time they have experienced multiple marriages to multiple people. Our tradition understands this phenomenon. Each person, say our Rabbis, "beholds seven worlds" and lives seven lives. Some of these stages are wonderful; he is a "king" at age one and "skips like a kid" at age ten. At other stages things get harder for him. At twenty he may feel a "longing for a wife," and as time passes he becomes like a donkey who is strained under the burden of providing for a family (*Ecclesiastes Rabbah* 1:2). Because our inner world is often shaped by our outer experiences, no one stays static. Just because we were happy yesterday does not mean we have to be today.

The only way to truly know another's pain is to ask. There is no right way to hurt. There is no expected approach to life's trials. We feel what is right for us at the moment. Yes, our tradition implores us to correct another's actions when they are destructive and dangerous. Our Torah commands us after all, "You shall surely reprove your neighbor" (Leviticus 19:17, translation mine). But we cannot confuse action with thought. Our inner world is ours alone, and radical acceptance of another's pain is the only avenue to radical connection.

Sometimes though, a person does not have the capacity to share. Our Rabbis warn us, "A person does not speak of his destitution except in the time of his ease" (*Ecclesiastes Rabbah* 1:12). Often, when others are in the deepest darkness, they lack the perspective to know to whom to turn. In those cases, the most important step we can take is to preempt their call and ask. Connection and knowledge are inextricably bound. We care by knowing, for without understanding we have no platform on which to act. Some people make it easy and share outright. Others are too guarded and will never let us in. But most people fall somewhere in the middle; they are waiting for an opening and ready to connect when we indicate that we will receive them without judgment.

There is a story that Rabbi Levi Yitzchak of Berdichev was once visiting the owner of a tavern in the Polish countryside. When he walked in, he saw two peasants at a table, gloriously drunk. Arms around each other, they were protesting how much they loved each other. Suddenly, Ivan turned to Peter: "Peter, tell me, what hurts me?" Bleary-eyed, Peter looked at Ivan. "How do I know what hurts you?" Ivan replied, disappointed, "If you don't know what hurts me, how can you say you love me?"[6]

Love is found in honest and open discovery of others. It exists when we uncover their secret and sacred yearnings. The Witch of En-dor could see that Saul was suffering and was receptive to his troubles. Nevertheless, I have no doubt that if Saul had not imploded, crestfallen with the news of his defeat, she would have asked. Then, receiving that information from him, she would have acted exactly the same way.

Empathy: The Pathway to Connection

Many millennia after the Witch of En-dor tended to Saul, Tolstoy created a character of equal depth and compassion. Gerasim, the simple and faithful servant in Tolstoy's short, yet profound work *The Death of Ivan Ilych*, does not move mountains, but his quiet dedication to his sick master Ivan Ilych is a model for all of those who seek to help others who suffer.

When he mysteriously falls ill, Ilych reaches out to those in his community. Despite his attempts at connection, however, his friends refuse to admit that he is dying. They instead focus on his illness and the possibility of recovery. They neither fully acknowledge his fears nor entertain his mortality. In ignoring the possibility of his death, no one engages with it. Ivan Ilych's concerns become unseen, and soon he internalizes that invisibility. Ilych feels no consolation from his community because their comfort is inadequate. Though they stand beside him in his physical pain, they ignore his emotional turmoil, and his sickness becomes a portal to alienation.

Gerasim, however, brings him the kind of comfort he seeks. Ilych's faithful servant sees his suffering for what it is, a precursor to death, and engages his master in conversation about his final days. He stays up all night, holding the ill man's feet and talking. In one episode, when Ilych is particularly unruly after a bad day, Gerasim responds with the words Ilych needs to hear: "We all die in our time. Why should I begrudge you a little sweat?"[7]

The reason Gerasim is successful in reaching his master is twofold. First, he is honest. He does not hide from the difficult reality in front of him. He knows that Ilych needs someone to acknowledge the possibility of death, and he steps into that role. But perhaps more importantly, Gerasim is empathetic. In the words of physician and award-winning author Atul Gawande in his book *Being Mortal*, "Gerasim sees that Ivan Ilyich is a suffering, frightened, and lonely man and takes pity on him, aware that someday he himself would share his master's fate."[8] By remembering his own mortality in the moment of confronting his master's, Gerasim stands beside Ivan Ilych in his suffering. He, in essence, says, "I know what it is like to know death will come. I feel it too. What you feel is real, and I understand."

Gerasim, like the Witch of En-dor, knows true empathy is the avenue to connection and avoids confusing it with its complicated step-child, sympathy. In a wonderful Internet short, Brené Brown, one of my favorite psychologists, examines the difference between these two personal approaches.

Brown uses the image of a person who is trapped in a deep hole for which there is no way out.[9] While we wish to help him escape, we lack the tools, the strength, and the resources to pull him from the chasm. While sympathy is peering down into the hole, giving advice, offering a few platitudes (i.e., it will get better, at least you have friends, I know someone who faced a similar challenge), and moving on, empathy is something much deeper. Those who practice empathy go down into the hole for a little while. *They know that while they cannot fix another's problem, it does not mean they should not dwell with them.* Those who are empathetic seek to walk for a little with others in their suffering. They tread alongside them, hand in hand through their darkness.

To practice true empathy, we need to channel our own painful past. We help a mourner by remembering our painful experiences of loss. We support the divorced by channeling our heartbreak. We comfort the lonely by recalling a time in our life when we were lonely as well. Though it is a powerful way to connect, carrying our former struggles is not easy. We have all faced a difficult period or an era of alienation that we would rather forget. But if we are truly to let others know that we understand them, if we are going declare to them that they are not alone in their loneliness, we have to allow ourselves to be vulnerable, opening ourselves up to experiences we wish we could erase.

Rebbe Nachman used to tell a story that explains the power of empathy. One day, in the largest kingdom in the land, the king's son suddenly decided that he was a rooster. He took off his princely robes, crawled under the table, and began squawking and eating only scraps. The king gathered all his wise men together and asked them for help. One by one, they approached the prince and did everything they could to convince the prince that he was still human. However, despite their best efforts, notwithstanding their cajoling, their pleading, and their best explanations, the prince remained convinced that he was a rooster.

Eventually, one rabbi in the kingdom devised a plan. Rather than speaking to the prince from above the table, he crawled under the table and started to act like a rooster himself. He too took off his clothes, got down on the floor, clucked, and began eating scraps. After a while, he paused and turned to the prince, "You know, you can be a rooster and still eat like a prince." Soon the prince was eating regular food. A short time later he turned to the prince, "You can also still be a rooster and dress like a prince." Open to the suggestion, the prince put on his princely robes. Finally, the rabbi said, "You can still be a rooster and come out from under the table." Immediately, the prince crawled out from under the table. Though in his heart he knew he would always be a rooster, the prince could now be part of society again. Because the rabbi had the courage to crawl under the table with him, he was able through thoughtful compassion to raise the prince up.

In the story, the other sages in the kingdom were sympathetic to the prince's plight. However, their sympathy didn't go far enough. Even if they understood the prince's desire to be a rooster, they conveyed an urgency for change that only left the prince feeling that they did not understand him. When the rabbi crawled under the table, he taught the prince that he had a kindred spirit. Showing others that we understand them gives them a sense of safety and promotes openness and trust. The rabbi never ordered the prince to emerge from under the table. He only helped him understand that when he was ready, it was safe to come out.

The rabbi in the story teaches us another important lesson: to be empathetic we don't need to fully embody another's pain; we just have to understand it. Unlike the prince, the rabbi had never felt the urge to become a rooster; however, something in his past prepared him to accept the prince when he did. Rarely do we know the exact struggles of those we seek to help. While I understand divorce, I have never lost a parent, dealt with unemployment, or struggled with aging. To be empathetic, however, we don't have to understand the full scope of another's pain. We just need to know what it is to hurt.

There is a powerful anecdote in our Talmud about Rabban Gamliel, who lived next door to a woman who lost her grown-up son. Like all forms of loneliness, there are aspects of this type of loss that are unique. In fact, our tradition says that of all forms of tears—tears caused by smoke, drugs, physical pain, or emotional exhaustion—tears brought about by the death of a grown-up child are the worst (*Lamentations Rabbah* 2:15). Rabban Gamliel had never lost an adult child. He was not fully knowledgeable of his neighbor's pain. However, our tradition says that hearing her voice, he was reminded of the destruction of the Temple. Channeling that pain, he began to weep alongside her "until his eyelashes fell out" (*Lamentations Rabbah* 1:24). For Gamliel, who had not lost a child, it could have been impossible for him to connect with her pain. However, remembering that he had hurt before, Gamliel knew that while pain may be specific, suffering is universal.

While we don't know what was going through the Witch of Endor's mind when Saul fell on his face, we do know that her response was like that of Gamliel, Gerasim, and all those who practice empathy. She approaches the king, dwelling with him in the midst of his despair, until he is ready to emerge.

Naming Pain While Not Comparing Tragedies

One of our greatest tools of comfort is the tool of naming. When we suffer, we often lack the ability to describe in words our specific experiences. We feel numb but don't know how to express it. We feel trapped but cannot articulate it. We feel lonely but don't want to admit it. As a rabbi, I was taught to help people tell their truth, to put into words what I heard them say and help them determine their lexicon of suffering. And though I do this professionally, what I am about to describe will work just as well if you are talking to a parent, coworker, child, or friend.

To help others speak their truth, I often have to articulate what I see them feeling. Are they alienated or angry, lost or isolated? Once I determine their truth, I have to speak up and take the risk in articulating their story. "Based on what you've just told me," I might say, "it sounds like you are feeling lonely." More often than not, I am correct, but even when I'm not, I have never faced anger for being wrong. People will give others the benefit of the doubt when they are trying. Usually if I miss the right word, I might hear, "Not exactly lonely ... more like no one understands me." Then, I have an opening to find the right word.

Unfortunately, while everyone needs to hear their truth, not everyone can provide enough clues to help us articulate it for them. In those cases, we need to draw on our empathy and take a guess. Our life experience becomes the well we draw from. Like Rabban Gamliel, who channeled the destruction of the Temple, we too can invoke our personal tragedies during these conversations to convey understanding. "Whenever I am sick, I often feel ambushed by the pain. Is that how you are feeling?" In one simple sentence I have given them an opening. If their experience matches mine, they feel understood. If different, it gives me a place to start moving toward their truth.

There is a risk to this, however. Unless we speak from our own experiences, lack judgment, and end with a question, it's easy for us to come off as if we know their pain. Empathy is feeling the pain of others, not presuming to be an expert in it. Just because I was sick doesn't mean I know what their sickness is like. I may have experienced being single, married, and divorced, but I have not been on their dates, slept in their bed, and been part of their arguments. Life experiences are captured in poetry, not textbooks, for a reason; our stories are too complex to yield anything but an impression.

Nevertheless, we can't be afraid to speak words of truth and love. Be audacious in your explorations. Name what you think another is feeling. If you do, you authenticate their pain. There are ways to deal with anger, fear, sadness, and loneliness. The first step to devising a plan to cope is to understand exactly what is causing the suffering in the first place. Without others to name what they see, those who suffer may never find the opportunity to take this first step.

The Challenge of Cheering Up

There is a fine line between being affable and whimsical, comforting and belittling. As a rabbi, I have always avoided the temptation to cheer up those who are suffering. To those in pain, the pressure from another to feel better is highly problematic. It adds stress to an already stressful time. Those who attempt to feel better and cannot, may feel they are failing you, while those who do, may learn to rely on others for the strength they could have cultivated themselves. When we try to cheer them up, we may also give them the message that their pain is not welcome or justified. It further stigmatizes those who are alone, forcing them to hide their authentic feelings.

Yet, Jewish tradition puts a premium on the act of cheering up others. Writing about adversity, the tenth-century scholar Rabbi Nissim tells the Talmudic tale of Rabbi Baroka, who one day met the prophet Elijah in the marketplace.[10] As they conversed, two men passed by them. Pointing at them, Elijah proclaimed that this duo deserves the highest reward in the world to come. Intrigued, Rabbi Baroka ran after them and asked them for their professions. He soon learned that they were jesters. "We cheer the grieving soul," they proclaimed, "and when we see someone whose heart is aching, we keep on diverting him and talking to him of things that would cheer him and dispel his sadness, until his dark mood leaves him."

This text poses an obvious tension. How can we both laud these jesters with a place in heaven for their work while knowing full well that for some, jokes and levity are some of the poorest tools in alleviating suffering? Wrestling with this text, many generations later, the great Hasidic master the Baal Shem Tov sought to understand the place of these jesters among the suffering.[11] For the Baal Shem Tov, there is meaning in suffering. There are enduring lessons in loss, alienation, and loneliness. When we are in the midst of our agony, however, it's hard to see these lessons. When we hurt, it's nearly impossible to see anything outside of ourselves. Levity, the Baal Shem Tov teaches, lifts us just enough outside of our bubble of pain that we might begin to see our struggles from a new, wider perspective and through this begin to heal.[12]

As wise as the Baal Shem Tov's teaching is, I think there is something else at play when these jesters do their work. Each of us values attributes of ourselves and views parts of our personalities with pride. Many of us see ourselves as kind and wise, thoughtful and hardworking.

For many, words like funny, positive, joyful, and spirited might easily top our list when we seek to describe ourselves. The deeper we grow in pain, however, the harder it is for us to acknowledge these things. Some psychologists have even likened this struggle to the phenomenon of trying unsuccessfully to remember a song while listening to another.[13] In both the case of our sadness and the case of music, our brains are so engaged in a task similar to the one we need them for that their bandwidth is too full to do both. We can only feel so much at a given time, which is why when we are sad, it's impossible to even imagine what happiness can be like. The job of the jesters isn't to belittle our sorrows. Instead they are trying, for a moment, to turn the pain off, as when we close our eyes to better remember an image, so we can recall the parts of ourselves that we have lost. In their presence we recover pieces of our soul long hidden, our positivity and joyfulness, our levity and vitality. Then, when they leave and we return to our pain, we can bring a vision to our suffering of who we want to be when we heal.

Becoming an Advocate for Others

In addition to giving our comfort and support to others when they reach out, often acting on others' behalf can send a clear signal that they are not alone. Part of what makes us feel lonely is sensing that no one shares our problems. If no one comes to our aid when we hurt, perhaps they do not truly understand our struggle. Feeling misunderstood can only deepen our alienations. When we suffer, we need an advocate.

Our tradition has numerous examples of people who have served as loving and supportive advocates for those who are lonely. There is a little-known tradition about Miriam, Moses's sister, that can teach the power of advocacy. According to Rabbinic tradition, Miriam was quite close to her sister-in-law, Tzipporah, who married Moses when he lived in Midian. Although their marriage started off strong, Moses soon pulled away from his wife.

Moses understood that when one hears the word of God, he or she must be pure. Sexual relations are integral to any relationship, but they invalidate a person's prophetic ability. This is why the men of Israel were told to stay away from their wives for the three days leading up to the giving of the Ten Commandments (Exodus 19:15). Unlike the rest of the people, however, Moses's term of prophecy was not finite. Because God could appear to him at any time, Moses was forced to stay away from Tzipporah indefinitely (*Tanchuma, Tzav* 13).

Though she was private about the increasing distance with her husband, Tzipporah could not fully hide her pain. According to Rabbinic lore, Miriam suspected that something was wrong in her brother and sister-in-law's marriage. She noticed that where once Tzipporah wore jewelry and linens, over time she had abandoned that style. When she asked about the change, Tzipporah told her that it no longer mattered to Moses (*Sifrei* on Numbers, chapter 99).

However, the real revelation came when two Israelites, Eldad and Medad, one day received the gift of prophecy. While others met these seers with fear and awe, Tzipporah viewed their gift with pity. She knew how difficult their new role would be for those who loved them. "Woe to their wives," she said. "They will be prophets, and they will withdraw from their wives, as my husband withdrew from me" (*Tanchuma, Tzav* 13). Miriam overheard her cry and knew that Tzipporah was suffering.

Rather than simply being a supportive ear and a comforting presence, Miriam decided to become Tzipporah's advocate. Many of us know the story in the book of Numbers, when Miriam criticizes her brother for marrying a Cushite woman. Many also know what happens next; because of her callous gossip, Miriam is punished by God with the ancient skin disease called *tzaraat* (Numbers 12). However, what many do not realize is that our tradition considers the designation of "Cushite" to be a code word for Tzipporah; just as Cushite women were distinctly beautiful, so too was Tzipporah (*Tanchuma, Tzav* 13).[14]

Overhearing Tzipporah's cries, Miriam speaks out. She wants Moses to understand what he is doing to his wife. "Your wife is a catch," she is seeming to say. "She is unique and beautiful, but yet you have withdrawn from her. Remember why you loved her in the first place and return to her."

In the end, Miriam wasn't successful. Moses did not return to his wife. In fact, Miriam was cast out to the wilderness soon after for challenging him. But we can imagine that Tzipporah, lonely from her husband's abandonment, would have heard of Miriam's efforts and at the very least known that someone understood her plight and cared enough about her to try to fix it.

Today, there are so many in our community who are in need of an ally. For those who are victims of hate, persecution, or neglect, having another stand up for you matters. Miriam's story is a challenge for all allies to be passionate advocates for others. Whether we stand up to a classmate's bully, advocate for a raise to a coworker's boss, or work to repair a friend's broken relationship, our voices matter. In a way, it almost isn't important what the results are. Miriam did not succeed in bringing Moses and Tzipporah together. Nevertheless, because she spoke up, Tzipporah knew she was not completely alone in her struggle. She had a partner in pain.

We all have the power to help those who are lonely. Our compassion is innate. It is in our DNA, because it was one of the building blocks of the world (Psalm 89:3). Whether we take inspiration from the Witch of En-dor, Miriam, Rabban Gamliel, or any of the other loving models of our tradition, our sacred texts reiterate time and again that we hold in our hands the precious gift of love. Whether and how we use it is entirely up to us.

9

The Communal Response to Loneliness

What We Can Do to Create Communities of Openness and Connection

One of the most tragic stories of the Bible surrounds a character who is unnamed. Mentioned only briefly in the book of Leviticus and called by the epithet "the blasphemer," students of Torah know his story well (Leviticus 24:10–23). One day, this man curses God. We do not know the exact nature of the curse, only that it is highly offensive. Not knowing what to do, Moses approaches God to receive instruction; God tells him to take the man outside of the camp and stone him to death in front of the whole community. Blasphemy will not be tolerated, and this man will become an example.

On the surface, the man's sin is easily understood. Someone loses control and becomes angry at heaven, upsetting the cosmos. He does the unspeakable and receives punishment. Yet, a closer look at the blasphemer's story yields a very different tale. Although we don't know his name, the Torah tells us the name of one of his parents. The blasphemer's mother is Shelomith, the daughter of Dibri the Dannite, and it is through these relationships that we learn a piece of his story. According to a midrash, Shelomith bore the blasphemer through an illicit union with an Egyptian taskmaster. Though some midrashim see her as complicit in the union (*Leviticus Rabbah* 32:5), others see her actions as accidental (*Exodus Rabbah* 1:28), and still others see her as the victim (*Pirke D'Rabbi Eliezer* 47), one thing holds true in all of these stories: without an Israelite father, Shelomith's son lacks a place in the community.

There is a famous story about the hours leading up to blasphemer's outburst (*Leviticus Rabbah* 32:2). Because his status is ambiguous—he is only half-Israelite—and because the Israelites pitch their tents with their father's tribe, he has no natural home. His mother's tribe of Dan does not see him as equal. His father is not one of them. He is tribe-less; he has no place. He takes them to court, but it is to no avail (*Sifra* 14:1–2). Moses does not accept him and even labels him as a *mamzer*, a term connoting a person who can never fully enter Israelite society.[1]

The blasphemer's story is tragic because he is left with no choice. His society has created barriers that keep him out. He is neither fully Egyptian nor fully Israelite. His loneliness is caused by callous policies that promote those on the inside and keep the outsider separate. He wants to belong. He yearns to assimilate, but the law will not acquiesce. So, angry and bitter, he curses God, the source for these unfair laws.

The case of the blasphemer teaches us a crucial lesson: as important as it might be to reach out to individuals, to hear their cry and answer their call, unless we make an effort to create a society that removes roadblocks to connection, we will always be fostering a culture of loneliness. Too many of us are stuck in the kind of impossible situations the blasphemer faced, those that incubate isolation and solitude. We have the power to change this.

Being Open to Those Who Are Looking for Their Place

The blasphemer's story is not unique. Our tradition warns us harshly about excluding those who wish to make inroads into our community.

Looking at the forgotten character of Timna, who was concubine to Eliphaz, Esau's son, the Rabbis imagine an equally heartbreaking story.

After seeing the wonders performed by the patriarchs and the power of the Jewish community, Timna, who is a royal princess, seeks out Abraham, asking to convert. When he rebuffs her, she finds Isaac, but he too denies her request. Moving on, she finds Jacob, but her pleas fall on deaf ears. None will accept her into their people (Talmud, *Sanhedrin* 99b). Despite the fact that she is wholehearted and passionate, they ignore her desire to enter into their camp. Hoping that if she is around them for long enough, they will accept her, she decides to become the concubine to Eliphaz, Esau's son. Perhaps her proximity to Jacob's tribe will create inroads to enter it.

However, her effort proves fruitless. They will not accept her. She is left without the attachment she so desires. Eventually, Timna gives birth to a child named Amalek, who would grow up to be the mortal enemy of the Jewish people and would attack them while they wandered in the desert post-Exodus. Asking many generations later why Amalek was permitted to cause Israel so much pain and anguish, the Rabbis respond that his existence was punishment for our ancestor's scorning of Timna.

Timna was looking for community and connection. She was hoping to find meaning and faith. But instead of accepting her with open arms and full hearts, our ancestors turned her aside. They failed to see the fundamental beauty that was at the heart of her request. There is an idiom in Judaism, *Midah k'neged midah*, translated loosely as "What goes around comes around" (*Mishnah Sotah* 1:7). As punishment, our ancestors were given a dose of their own medicine. Because they excluded someone looking for a connection to community, they were given an enemy who sought to destroy their community's connection.

In Timna's story, we find a crucial lesson: if someone wants to join your community, you must not stand in their way. Even if the answer is complicated, figure out a way to say yes. Hillel famously accepted a student who agreed to convert if he could recite the whole Torah for him while standing on one foot. While impossible, he answered yes, and then coined the adage "What is hateful to you, do not do to your neighbor" (Talmud, *Shabbat* 31a). Then, he continued, challenging him. "The rest of the Torah is commentary," he said, "so go study."

Today there are too many barriers for entry into our communities, some explicit and some implicit. While there are certainly more than can possibly be examined here, a few emblematic examples from my own experience as a rabbi might serve to explain how to avoid leading people toward alienation.

For many communities, policies around interfaith families are alienating and make full participation in synagogue life impossible. Like Timna, these families arrive excited about belonging, only to get the message that by marrying someone they love, they have stepped outside of a communal norm and are not welcome. There are synagogues that will not include the non-Jewish member's name on mailings, give them leadership positions in the community, or honor them during family celebratory moments like baby namings. Though many of these family members may not celebrate other faiths and are active and integral forces in raising Jewish children, they are treated as invisible to the community. They want to belong, but all too often our policies make their belonging impossible. This only reinforces their isolation. The community that could have alleviated their loneliness has now exacerbated it.

Cost can also be a barrier. For many of us, the promise of instant community is tantalizingly close. We know that this school, this club, or this synagogue might provide shared experiences and meaningful relationships if only we could afford to join. Even though many communities offer scholarships or price breaks, many of us do not want to ask for them or feel humiliated filling out the forms needed to receive the funds. Someone who is lonely may feel even more alienated if they are made to feel separate from a group because they need to ask for help. We need models in our community like Rav Huna of many generations ago, who used to suspend a water jug full of medicine at his lintel and proclaim, "Whoever needs it, let him come and take of it" (Talmud, *Taanit* 20b). Yes, our organizations must figure out funding models to sustain themselves, but we need to lead with messages of openness rather than place, foremost, the stumbling block of finances. We need to convey that every searcher can find a home here.

I've always admired the story of Hillel, who knew the importance of openness and acceptance because he was on the outside as a youth. There is a story (Talmud, *Yoma* 35b), told by our Rabbis, that one day Hillel did not have enough money to pay for his daily studies. Showing up anyway, he was cast out of the study hall. Angry, Hillel refused to accept defeat. He climbed on to the roof of the building and peered in through the skylight, listening to the lecture below. That night it snowed, but Hillel was so enthralled by the class that he forgot to come down, and he fell asleep under the snow. The next day, the students noticed a strange shadow cast above them. Looking up toward the skylight, they saw Hillel. They found him cold and weak and brought him into the study hall. Realizing his dedication, the rabbis of the community waived the fee and made it possible for him to join. From that day on, Hillel found a place in the community and rose to become one of the greatest rabbis of his generation.

Another group often disenfranchised are families where one or more members have a disability. A diverse congregation will have a diversity of members. Some will be blind, others deaf, others in wheelchairs, and still others will have children who need extra support to succeed in school. Communities who claim not to have many people who fall into these categories are probably so out of touch with the needs of their community that those with disabilities have just stopped trying to come altogether. Until recently, our congregation did not do programming for children with special needs. Before this, and on more than one occasion, I remember the shock and shame of learning that a child I had gotten to know in religious school had a brother or a sister with special needs who I did not know existed. Because we did not have a place for them in our school, they never came around. What message are we sending to families when we fully embrace one child while acting as if the other does not exist? Likewise, how can we tell someone with a physical disability that we want them as part of our community while not providing a ramp for them to make it to services or a book that has large enough print for them to read? Like Timna, they are knocking on our door asking for acceptance and love, but by our inaction, we too often turn them away.

Openness to interfaith families, those with disabilities, and those struggling with finances are just three examples of how we can break down barriers, but there are certainly more. Do we use technology that our older members cannot understand? Does our programming exist at only one time so that parents of young children must choose between attending class and putting their kids to bed? Does our schedule force our older members to venture out at night, when they cannot see hidden patches of ice? Do we have changing tables in both the men's and women's rooms, so any parent can bring their baby to synagogue? If communal connection is one remedy to the plague of loneliness, perhaps we should examine our barriers, both explicit and implicit, so we can greet the seeker with openness and affirmation.

Discarding Shibboleths

The Bible tells the story of Jephthah, who commanded an army of a group called the Gileadites (Judges 12:1–7). At the time, his army was in conflict with a group from the tribe of Ephraim. Though he sought to defeat them, one factor stood in his way: he could not distinguish his men from theirs. Jephthah developed a plan to tell the two groups apart. He knew that those who were raised with an Ephraimite tongue had not developed the ability to distinguish the "sh" sound from the "s" sound. Those who could pronounce the word *shibboleth*, an ancient Hebrew word for a bundle of wheat, were from his kin, but those who could only pronounce *sibboleth* had to be other. That day, Jephthah used his tactic to identify forty-two thousand Ephraimites and defeat them outright.

Taking its inspiration from this biblical account, the word "shibboleth" has made its way into the English lexicon, though today it has a much broader meaning. A shibboleth is anything that functions as a litmus test to distinguish who is part of the "inside group" and who is on the outside. As it was for Jephthah, it could be linguistic, but it also can be insider dress, food, or values.

While boundaries are important in defining a group, all too often we are indiscriminate about our use of shibboleths. Those who are wealthy make reference to experiences to which their poorer counterparts cannot relate. We make assumptions that our immigrant brothers and sisters will understand the fundamental ethos of America, but we do not educate them on it. Members of a given generation reminisce about what they watched or what was on the radio when they were younger and are surprised when those who are of a different generation cannot participate.

Sadly, the Jewish community is a major culprit in abusing shibboleths. Judaism is such a multifaceted faith that it contains countless moments that separate insiders from outsiders. Unlike the above examples, these shibboleths are not barriers to participation per se. They are much more insidious. They allow anyone to show up but make them leave feeling like there will never be a place for them in the community.

Since rabbis speak with the authority of tradition and many of our congregants do not have our knowledge of Torah, our religious analysis of political policy can feel authoritative. If we are genuine, we know that our tradition is ripe with tensions that make policy stands difficult. Our tradition wavers between caring for the other and watching out for ourselves, between the needs of humanity and the needs of the natural world, between the prophetic and the pragmatic voice. In an effort to create a good sermon, however, we don't always unpack these tensions. When we don't represent the full scope of Jewish thought, we risk preaching the gospel of political liberalism or conservatism. Since most of our congregants cannot quote text back to us, we risk labeling their views as un-Jewish and their voice in our communal conversation as marginal. We create a false dichotomy between their ethics and their religion, and we drive them away.

Like politics, God too can serve as a shibboleth. No person has a monopoly on religious truth. Yet, how often do we make statements about God that divide the congregation? Do we use gendered language, which alienates those who cannot see God as male? Do we treat God as a person, leaving no room for God as spirit or force? Do we ascribe acts to God that make it impossible for many in our congregation to believe? An open congregation honors the struggle of those who attend. Like the Ephraimites, there are those who just cannot say what is expected of them about God. If that is the case, perhaps our expectations are misplaced. By not honoring their views and encouraging their explorations, we only serve to drive them farther from the community.

Another important shibboleth in our community appears when we employ the word "we" into our discourse. When we speak with nostalgia about our common history, is it mainly out of a German / Eastern European ethos? When we speak about "our kids" or "us, as parents," do we also acknowledge that there are some who are unable to have children in our midst? Do we throw around Yiddish terms that we do not define because we assume that it is a shared cultural language? Do we have both grape juice and wine to make sure that those who cannot drink can share in the joy of Shabbat *Kiddush?*

Shibboleths can drive a wedge between people and their community. They reinforce all our insecurities about not belonging and never connecting. If those who are lonely need radical acceptance, then we have to be careful that we aren't silently signaling to them that they will always be on the outside.

Creating Advocacy Movements

Let's return to Moses. For forty years, Moses led the people through the desert. Yet, despite his faithfulness and service to God, he was unable to enter the Promised Land. Moses had erred at the waters of Meribah, losing control of his anger and disobeying God's instructions, and because of these actions, he was condemned to die in the desert. He would see the Land of Israel but would never tread on its soil.

What made this punishment so lonely for Moses was not its substance, but rather the reaction of the people to it. According to the Midrash, God's decree that Moses would not enter the Promised Land was not final. With a bit of advocacy from the people, Moses would be allowed to continue. Our tradition likens God to a king who has divorced his wife (Moses) and plans to remarry (*Deuteronomy Rabbah*

3:11). Learning of the king's plan, his ex-wife summons her children and begs them to intervene on her behalf. "Are you really going to accept her?" she asks of their future stepmother, hoping they will agree to intervene. Instead of siding with her, however, they simply answer "yes." Dejected, she is forced to endorse the new queen.

The parallel here is obvious. God has chosen Joshua to be the new leader of the Israelites. Hoping the Jewish people would advocate for him, Moses is horrified to learn that they agree with God's decision. Another midrash imagines Moses's reaction when he realizes that he is alone. Recalling that forty years earlier, he had begged God not to destroy the Jewish people after they built the golden calf, Moses shouts, "One man saved six hundred thousand at the time of the golden calf, and yet six hundred thousand cannot save [but] one man" (*Deuteronomy Rabbah* 7:10).

Moses was in trouble. He had pleaded with God to change his fate, but God would not listen to him. He was powerless. Moses was crying out for the people's aid, but they ignored his plea. Imagine how different it might have been if the people organized to help their leader. What might it have been like if they marched to God and proclaimed in one voice to let Moses cross the Jordan at their side? Moses would have certainly felt supported. And he would have absolutely felt less isolated. What Moses needed was a movement.

Moses is a symbol to all those who need society's support. As important as it is to have individuals who speak out for you, as Miriam did for Tzipporah, letting you know you are not alone, often one of the most important things we can do for others' sense of alienation is to gather many voices to speak for them. Religious persecution, racial prejudice, sexism, and homophobia are as much engines of loneliness as death, sickness, or divorce. Our identity is bound and determined by the group to which we belong. When someone insults us because we are Jewish, black, or gay, they say to us, "We don't care who you actually are, only that you are a placeholder for a group we hate." But when a group of people rally around us, they send us the message, "You are a person. We see you. Your plight is our plight. And though I do not know you, I care about you."

One of the most powerful anecdotes in Ta-Nehisi Coates's master-ful meditation on race in America, *Between the World and Me*, surrounds a comment made by the mother of a murdered black teen to Coates's then thirteen-year-old son after her son was killed because he had refused to turn his music down. Looking at the boy, she stated emphatically:

> You exist. You matter. You have value. You have every
> right to wear your hoodie, to play your music as loud as
> you want. You have every right to be you. And no one
> should deter you from being you. You have to be you.
> And you can never be afraid to be you.[2]

These words are simple and profound. Yet, as important as it was for Coates's son to hear these words from one person, it is perhaps more important for society to convey to him these truths. Persecution can make people feel invisible. Standing beside their plight in full-voiced support and partnership, many voices united, we send the message to those struggling that we see them, they count, and we care.

The Israelite failure to do this for Moses does not have to be our failure. Whether advocating for just racial and economic policies, deal-ing with anti-Semitism on college campuses, or advocating for legisla-tion that ends workplace discrimination for the LGBT community, the ally voice matters. Movements matter. They are how society says, "We get it. You are not alone."

Creating Communal Moments of Triumph

Rallies, protests, and marches are one of the great tools of a movement. Many of us have stood in powerful communal gatherings and felt a part of something greater than ourselves. Our shared mission feels almost ordained. Yes, there are certainly times when crowds are alienating, but when done well, communities can form around a larger purpose, and everyone involved can find a voice in the cacophony.

I've spoken with many people who marched in Selma, participated in the Occupy Wall Street movement, and attended the inauguration of our first black president. All had the same experience. They felt like the crowd they were a part of was a living organism and they made up an important piece of it. They describe a unique energy to which they contributed and from which they benefited. And luckily, for those less politically inclined, their description matches other communal experiences that are easier to re-create.

Musical gatherings have a similar power to political rallies. Not every concert is transformative, but when it is, it has the power to unite a group of disparate individuals into a community of listeners. And some bands are better than others at this. When bands like Phish or the Grateful Dead lose themselves in the music, so do their fans. In an instant, all individual consciousnesses merge into a collective. For a brief time, all feel as one. The act of dancing, swaying, or singing takes on religious meaning. Because they no longer have a self, they cannot feel alone, and even this momentary release of loneliness can be enough to help a sufferer find a way out.

At its best, communal prayer imitates the mission of the rally and the spiritual unity of the concert. Though not every prayer service will be transformative, when a group of people trust one another enough to pour their hearts out together in song or silent meditation, it's possible for a sanctuary to come alive and spiritual unity to reign. I've been a part of these communities. They are fleeting, but when you are in them, your neighbors' prayers are yours, you share their heartache, your yearnings are combined. Your shared experience breaks down the walls that separate you and makes you and others one.

Literature can also function in a similar way. In a 2014 essay in the *New York Review of Books* entitled "Make This Not True," cultural critic Wyatt Mason explored the reasons why many enjoy reading the novelist David Foster Wallace.[3] Mason explains that many of us turn to literature to combat our loneliness. Though literature may have multiple approaches to answering our most fundamental questions about isolation and connection, Foster Wallace has a special place in answering this query, because David Foster Wallace is incredibly difficult to read. To make it through a book like *Infinite Jest* is a feat, which is why perhaps more than for any other author, Foster Wallace's readers are a community. When you finish his novel, you enter into an elite club of people who have struggled alongside you and prevailed, and though it may not sustain you forever, for at least a short while you are connected and feel less alone.

I have personally seen this same phenomenon with Jewish texts. The Talmud is notoriously hard. If it were simply written in the terse, dead Aramaic that it is, it would be difficult enough, but even after understanding the meaning of the words, one is still left with the legal give-and-take, the jumps in logic, and the dropped arguments that have frustrated Talmud students for centuries. Locally, there is something powerful about a class of students all struggling with the same texts together, relying on one another's insights and supporting one another through their textual journey.

Globally though, as it is for the readers of Foster Wallace, there is something profound about knowing that there are thousands of strangers out in the world who are struggling just as you are. There is a certain genius to the phenomenon of *Daf Yomi*, the program whereby everyone around the globe studies the same page of Talmud on the same day. We know we are not the only ones pushing ourselves to gain insights about which fuel we can use to light the Shabbat candles or when the appropriate time is to say the morning *Sh'ma* prayer. And when we finally do finish a tractate of study, we know that others like us have done the same.

Though the Talmud is certainly the closest example to Foster Wallace, it is not the only one. Like Jewish study, Jewish practice is not easy. The beauty of the Jewish calendar is that throughout the year, Jews struggle to obey the same laws at the same times. Like finishing a tractate of Talmud, those who survive a Yom Kippur fast, who turn down food that is not Kosher despite their craving for it, and who rush to morning prayer when they have a million other things to do share a connection and are part of a community. They have conquered the same demons within themselves that told them they could not make it through, that they should just have a bite or should roll over and go to bed. Jewish practice creates a kinship with all those in their community, known and unknown, whom they have struggled alongside. In that instant, they are part of something bigger.

Recognizing the Importance of Names

Community experiences work, but only if others create safe places for us to seek acceptance, and this begins with the way we address one another. According to Jewish tradition, the most intimate and respectful way we can call one another is by our given names.[4] Titles are important, but they create distance. Honor is bestowed by dropping those titles. There is a reason, our Rabbis tell us, that we call Moses "Moshe Rabbeinu" (Moses our teacher) and not "Rabbeinu Moshe" (our teacher, Moses). Moses had an identity before he was a teacher, and that identity should come first. When we truly honor another, the person supersedes the role rather than the role subjugating the person.[5]

I've been part of two kinds of communities: those that embrace the centrality of names and those that do not. When communities place names at the forefront, they foster deeper and more meaningful connections. This is because the longer we live, the more saturated with meaning our names become. The Israeli poet Zelda famously wrote that each of us has a name given to us by "our father and mother ... our smile ... our attire ... our friends"; by "our yearnings ... celebrations ... our work ... the seasons."[6] Our names are the vessels for our life experiences, and to be truly seen, our names need to be honored.

Perhaps this is one reason why there is a superstition in Judaism against counting people. None of us are numbers. It is our names that matter, for in them is our story. If loneliness is the result of not feeling seen, then the very first step of a community is make sure that others use our names. It ensures we do not disappear into the crowd. Every encounter we have should facilitate the simple act of learning and speaking another's name. Though smaller than many of the steps outlined above, it's the most basic avenue to connection and an easy reminder to us every time we are addressed that we matter.

There Is No Silver Bullet

Perhaps the most important factor linking each of these communal solutions to loneliness is that they are all insufficient. None, on their own, has much power to change our communal situation. Our loneliness is too ingrained and runs too deep. Yet, combined with the individual approaches of the previous chapter, the solutions in this chapter help form the building blocks we need to create a culture in our communities, both Jewish and secular, that will combat loneliness. The next chapter will discuss the hard work that we as individuals can do to help ourselves through our own struggles.

10

Sacred Searching

Finding God, Purpose, and Self in Times of Loneliness

Rabbi Nachman of Horodenka, the grandfather of Rabbi Nachman of Breslov, once told this story: A man washed up at the foot of a great city after his ship ran aground. As he approached the gates, all the townspeople rushed out to meet him. Immediately, he learned that he was to be crowned the king. He was dressed in royal garb, given the royal crown, and placed on the royal throne. Soon, his excitement turned to trepidation. He learned that the city chose a new king once every year. After his term was up, the king would be stripped of his royal robe and exiled to an island to live alone. He would be doomed to a life of misery and isolation, the foil of his year in power.

Seeking advice, the king developed a plan. While the rules of the kingdom dictated that at the moment of exile the king must leave all his wealth and power behind, he could send provisions and workers ahead well before his term was up. During his year in power he would plant the seeds, both literal and figurative, to ensure that his remaining days on the island would not be defined by loneliness and poverty. When the year was finished and he was deposed, the king retired to the island, but because of his advance planning he found there were ample supplies and numerous people waiting for him. Though he should have felt lonely, his foresight ensured he would live out his days in peace and at ease.[1]

The message of this story is simple: while you can't always ensure that times won't get tough, you can plan ahead so that when you end up in a place of desolation and alienation, what you need is waiting for you. As we think about what we need to cope with loneliness when it arises in our lives, we can do more than reach out to others and seek communities of openness and love, though both are crucial. To truly transcend loneliness, we need to cultivate certain virtues and skills within us that will give us the strength to persevere when we find ourselves on the island. The following chapter will examine three: a connection with God, our ability to be alone, and the search for purpose. Each of these three capacities are lights on which we can draw when we face our darkest hour.

God and Humanity: Fostering Sacred Connection

Throughout this book we have established two facts: God and humanity are both lonely, and both of us yearn for the other. For God, loneliness comes because humanity does not call out to their creator and refuses to search when God hides. For us, suffering without a cosmic partner further alienates us from a God we should seek out when these things happen. Like the king who sends supplies forward, however, we can work to cultivate a relationship with God so that when we are in our time of need, we can find God waiting and unite in our loneliness.

I've always admired the adage by the Hasidic rabbi Menachem Mendel of Kotzk, "Where is God? Wherever you let God in." God exists when we are open to the holiness around us. Often, however, we are not prepared to let God approach. Our guard is up. Life hardens us. We struggle to be open, to see God's fingerprints in the world.

If spirituality is a muscle, it can atrophy. Those that carry skepticism with them will struggle to find God when they are ready to look. But those who are accustomed to finding the spirit of God in everything will more easily find it when they are in need. The best way to learn to find God is to get good at the search. There is a fine line between doubt and wonder. Both involve uncertainty, but where doubt starts with a premise of negativity, wonder starts on a platform of openness.

If we are mystified at the beauty of nature, amazed at the face of a child, captured by the connection with a lover, and marveled by the heights of human potential, we are more able to see God in those moments and more able to re-create them when we yearn for divine connection.

We are not born with the capacity for divine connection. We have to cultivate it. Rabbi Jonathan Sacks understood this well.[2] Building off a statement by Maimonides, Sacks explains that the world is ripe with God's blessing and love. However, we cannot easily access it. He likens our situation to standing in the rain without a bucket to catch the drops. God is there, but we aren't ready. The goal, he says, is through prayer (and wonder) to turn ourselves into a container that can hold the rain. Only by the thoughtful and arduous task of changing ourselves can we weld our souls into vessels for godliness.

This is why, often, we pray but do not feel closer to God. Prayer is transformational, not transactional. It's meant to change us, not to change God. I've sat through so many services and felt nothing. I've prayed to the cosmos, fearing that my deepest yearnings would remain forever in the echo chambers of eternity. But later, when I needed it the most, I've stood atop a mountain or sat down with a friend and felt deeply connected to God. It was only then that I knew that if I had not encountered the moments of weariness and dissatisfaction, the ennui of the spiritual being, I would not have been ready and open to find God in the everyday.

Our religious loneliness comes from calling out to a God who does not seem to listen. But prayer is more than reaching out to the Other. Those who transcend alienation from God see themselves in relationship with the Divine. The primary verbs of religious connection are not asking or demanding, but meeting. If God yearns for the same connection we do, then the goal is to yearn together. Eventually our pains will unite and become one, and in that instance, for a brief time, our loneliness will be subsumed by a cosmic wholeness.

Our Rabbis understood just how patient we must be in order to finally connect with God (*Lamentations Rabbah* 2:30). As they have in so many other places, they liken God to a king who is forced to travel to a distant country for a long period of time. Before he goes, he gives his wife a document spelling out his commitment to her and describing her reward for waiting. As time passes, his wife becomes forlorn. She is desperately lonely without her husband. When she turns to her neighbors for comfort, they goad and vex her, "The king has left you, gone away to a distant country, and will never return to you." But when she reaches the nadir of her sorrow, she goes into her room and reads the king's promise. Only then does she have the strength to move forward.

Eventually, the king returns home. Seeing that his wife has remained faithful to him after these many years, he asks her how she was able to wait for him. "When I felt like you would never return," she says, "I took out your promissory note. Without it, I would not have had the strength to persevere and would have long ago given up hope."

So too, say our Rabbis, the Jewish people face a God who is hidden. God is far from us, and we do not know when God will return to our midst. But we too have a sacred document. We have the wisdom of our Torah, which informs the yearnings of our prayer book and the sacred rhythm of Jewish practice. And though our religious life may not immediately bring God into our midst, it can remind us that one day God may return home. When we learn, when we pray, when we open ourselves to the sparks of divinity around us, we gain the strength to push through our loneliness. And then one day God reappears, and we haven't left; we are still waiting because Judaism is a gift that holds us together through our alienation. And God too looks at us with incredulity, laughing, "You waited for me after all these years?"

Learning to Embrace Aloneness

As we established earlier in the book, there is a difference between being lonely and being alone. Loneliness can happen in crowds, while conversely we can feel whole in solitude. As separate as these two phenomena may seem, however, the two indeed are linked. Loneliness is caused in part by feeling forced into aloneness. Plenty of people enjoy a Saturday night by themselves, but isolation and alienation follow when we wish we had plans and settle for a night in.

I remember after my divorce the anxiety that would overcome me when I thought about my empty apartment. I remember that a unique storminess in my chest would form by three o'clock if I had not secured a late-night drink with a friend or found the occasion to go on a date. The prospect of spending a night alone with my thoughts was horrifying to me. The ability to be alone must be nurtured. I had never cultivated that practice, and so when I was forced to face solitude, I was doomed to loneliness.

Today, fewer people than ever feel comfortable being alone. Technology has provided an escape hatch from ourselves. We can never be far from people if they are only a fingertip away. When we begin to feel lonely, we obscure our pain with social media and text messaging, which serve as diversions from the hard work of facing our thoughts. Even if we use our phones for other purposes, podcasts and playlists distract from self-reflections that could blossom if we gave them space to flower. Some of our loneliest moments appear at times when we have no digital Band-Aids, when we are driving, on a subway, or in a boring meeting. So since there is no escape from ourselves, it's all the more important to carve out intentional time to confront our inner musings and foster an appreciation for solitude.

Plenty of people assume that meditation will solve our inability to be alone. If we could only close our eyes and concentrate on our breath, we could nurture our inner world. But meditation without its accompanying philosophy is futile. I once heard it explained that the reason meditation is so difficult is because as soon as we turn off the noise of the outside world, we will find ourselves "locked in a phone booth with a crazy person, screaming into a megaphone."

The purpose of meditation is not to force ourselves to be alone. It is instead meant to teach us not to judge ourselves when we are. Good meditation works like this: We pick a stimulus, maybe the coldness of the breath as it enters our nostrils, maybe the transition point between emptying our lungs and beginning to fill them, and we concentrate on it. Then, as always happens, our mind wanders. A few minutes later we realize that we have spent a significant amount of time on the laundry list of tasks and concerns in our lives. We have lost the breath. When we realize we have strayed, we have two options. We can punish ourselves for wandering, describing our worth as "bad meditators" and judging our thoughts as distracting and inconvenient, or we can simply notice that we have wandered and return to the breath. Meditation is that act of teaching ourselves non-judgment and internal kindness. And though it's a pretty good way, there are other ways to do this as well.

Whether we journal or pray, whether we would prefer to sit in meditation or on a therapist's sofa, one of our chief tasks to combat loneliness is to learn to be with ourselves. How many of us are our own worst enemy? How many of us forgive others while critiquing those same traits within? I don't want to be stuck on a Saturday night with someone I don't like. I want to be surrounded by warmth and compassion, goodwill and devotion. If we don't learn to feel this for ourselves, if our mantra for self-care is judgment before forgiveness, criticism over pride, then time without others will remain forever excruciating.

There is holiness to solitude. Most people have no trouble seeing God's presence in acts of interpersonal connection. We quote thinkers, like Martin Buber and Emmanuel Levinas, who speak about the power of embracing the other. Part of the reason we love these ideas is that we know the oft-quoted teaching that we were created b'tzelem Elohim, "in the image of God" (Genesis 1:27). Sadly, while it's easy for us to acknowledge the godliness of others, it's much harder for us each to accept it in ourselves. If only we could remember the teaching by Rabbi Joshua ben Levi: each of us has a choir of angels that process before us proclaiming, "Make way for the image of God!" (Deuteronomy Rabbah 4:4).

The chief obstacle to noticing our inherent self-worth is the mistaken notion that it lies in something else. How many of us attach our happiness to an object? Whether our money, our jobs, our fame, or our looks, we too often invest things out of our control with the power to dictate our joys. The reason it is so problematic to give power to these things is that they can fail us. Looks and fame can fade, money can dry up, careers can end. When they do, our smokescreen vanishes. We are left raw and wanting, looking to patch up the hole that formed when they disappeared.

People too can function like fame or money. Most of us know that an unhealthy obsession with an individual can hurt us, but fewer consider that we face the same risk when we invest power with people as a whole. The presence of others should enrich our lives, not determine it. When we don't like ourselves, we too often turn to friends and family to show us why we matter. We ordain their love and attention with the power to sustain us or destroy us. We assume that as long as they accept our faults and blemishes, we don't have to do the hard work of confronting them ourselves. But people disappear. If everything we know about ourselves is mediated through the eyes of another, we can't help but grope blindly when they are gone.

Lucky for us, the more deliberate time we spend alone, inventorying our virtues and celebrating our dignity, the easier it will get. Time alone is self-perpetuating. It gets easier until it becomes a gift, providing us the space to mine, in solitude, our internal recesses and encounter sanctity within. And when we do, we will have divorced aloneness from its stepchild loneliness and come one step closer to wholeness. All we need is the courage to step into the phone booth and learn to love who we find there.

The Search for Purpose and Meaning

I've often found that the people who are best able to transcend loneliness often have a sense of purpose that accompanies a desire for companionship. They live out the edict put forth by the nineteenth-century philosopher Friedrich Nietzsche, "He who has a Why to live for can bear almost any How."[3] People come and go. Friends disappoint, lovers detach, and parents die. Purpose and meaning abide.

We all connect to different facets of life. Some of us are on a sacred mission to heal the broken world. We seek to feed the poor, support the fallen, comfort the bereaved. Others yearn to create. We make art, craft music, and add beauty to the world. Still others seek to serve God. Our avenue of connection may be prayer, study, or mitzvot. Whatever the source, mission gives our lives meaning and our deeds direction.

When we are able to point to purpose in our lives, we dull the pain of people. We invest our lives with something greater than any single relationship can give. I've seen firsthand the salvific power of mission. After my grandfather died, my grandmother channeled her grief into volunteering at the local senior center. When one of my congregants dealt with infertility issues, she sought increasing visibility around the epidemic. When a woman I knew sent her last child to college, she learned to chant Torah and became a regular on Saturday morning. After my divorce, I was carried by the notion that through serving my community as a rabbi, I could bring them closer to God and one another.

Though many times in this book we have cautioned against solving loneliness through attending more social events and programming, mission-driven activities are different. The senior center was ancillary to my grandmother; after experiencing loss, she was simply looking for a place to funnel her love. For my congregant, the Torah class was secondary to the pursuit of Jewish knowledge and the exploration of spirituality. Chanting was just an avenue. In both of these cases, we could replace the specific activity with a host of others, and they would have been just as meaningful; in a life of purpose the vehicle is almost always subservient to the goal.

The goal of life is to live with purpose, and to do this we must give to others. Our Rabbis understood this. They explained, "A baby enters the world with hands clenched, as if to say, 'The world is mine; I shall grab it.' A person leaves with hands open, as if to say, 'I can take nothing with me'" (Ecclesiastes Rabbah 5:14). When we are young, everything seems to be ours. We want the whole world in our hands. And then, life disappoints us. We realize that the universe is large and we are not at its center. Our first mission, the need to grab everything, is misplaced. To revise our mission, we must do the opposite. Living a truly fulfilled life means emptying our hands, leaving nothing on the table. It means making the world better than we found it, leading with compassion, healing the brokenness around us, and conveying joy.

Too many people wait to search for purpose until they find themselves in the depths. They think that if they could only find their mission, they could heal their loneliness. Mission doesn't work like that. If we bind our sense of purpose to an outcome like personal healing or self-discovery, our mission becomes a thing we may evaluate rather than a duty we can pursue. If I love in the hopes of its return, my love can be in vain. If I love simply because you are, then my act of loving is enough.

It's hard to step outside ourselves when we suffer. True giving is nearly impossible when we need so much. Some can find purpose in the midst of pain and should try. But for most of us who can't, purpose and meaning can and should be nurtured before we hurt, at times before we are tempted to use them for triage when we are in crisis. They are perhaps the best supplies that we can send forward to that island for when we will inevitably arrive.

Growing from Our Loneliness

Often when we suffer it seems purposeless. However, just because there is no grand meaning to our pain doesn't mean we can't grow from it. While there is little that is good *about* loneliness, there is still good that blossoms *from* it. Though we may not know it at the time, when we suffer, we are cultivating the exact virtues in ourselves others may need when they find themselves in the same place we are: understanding and experience, wisdom and compassion. Having journeyed through pain, we are better equipped to perceive another's hurt, to identify it, and to accept it, and then to share our experiences to help guide them toward healing.

Our suffering has purpose only insofar as it can be repurposed. Our tradition understands this well. In the Torah, after facing a rebellion by Korach and his men, Moses sets up a test. They will each offer sacrifices to God in fire pans. As each party lights their incense, a fire leaps up from some of the pans and consumes many of Korach's followers (Numbers 16:35). After the carnage subsides, God commands Eleazar the priest to collect the fire pans and hammer them into plates to cover the sacred altar. In addition to serving as a warning for future generations not to rebel, these plates were holy now. God had touched them, and they deserved a holy platform. The thing that had meant destruction to so many would mean protection for the altar, the most sacred of spaces.

For the Israelites, these fire pans were scars. They were everlasting reminders of the pain of rebellion. Unable to rid themselves of them because of their divine connection, they had three choices. They could hide them, they could display them, or they could reimagine them. While hiding the plates could keep them out of sight, this plan had one fundamental flaw. From time to time, especially when the nomadic Israelites would pack up and move onward, they would be discovered and all the pain of rebellion would come flooding back. Conversely, if they displayed them, there would be no secrecy, but their presence in the camp would become oppressive. But repurposed, the plates could hold two meanings: they would be a reminder of the past while serving a useful role in the present.

Many of us have felt destroyed by loneliness, and many of us have survived. Like the Israelites, we too carry scars with us. And like them we have three choices. We can hide our pain, knowing that from time to time a trigger will come that will place us back in our loneliness. We can display it, wearing our history on our sleeve but not fully moving on. Or we too can repurpose it. We can make sharing our story and using it to heal others into a sacred mission. We can embrace others as we wished we were embraced. We can use our suffering to engender empathy and conjure compassion. We can use our embittered past to better the lives of others. Like the fire pans, our suffering is holy because we are holy. Every experience of our God-touched lives matters.

Emily Dickinson once wrote:

> If I can stop one heart from breaking
> I shall not live in vain;
> If I can ease one life the aching,
> Or cool one pain,
> Or help one fainting robin
> Unto his nest again,
> I shall not live in vain.[4]

We don't have to suffer for naught. Though our loneliness seems purposeless, we can endow it with purpose. We can hammer our heartache into a covering for another's soul.

Conclusion
The Seeds of Redemption and the Roots of Hope

For thirty-five hundred years, the Jewish people have emphasized one fundamental theme in our prayers, myths, and teachings: redemption is possible and ongoing. Our story is not yet over. True, we once found ourselves burdened by trouble in a foreign land, and God heard our cries, taking us from slavery to freedom. But the darkness and doubt, fear and fatigue that we found in Egypt was not a one-time occurrence. These things appear daily.

Today we need redemption as much as we ever have. Though many seek redemption from external ills—the diseases of hate, bigotry, racism, and war—many others struggle with a darkness within. This darkness can be just as insidious. It is a different kind of slavery. We are prisoners of self. Our crime is simple. We are victims of our losses, our doubts, and our shame. Separated from the rest of the world, loneliness is our only companion.

For those suffering from loneliness, it too often seems that there is no hope. Nothing can be further from the truth. Everyone can find redemption.

When the Jews went down to Egypt, the Torah counts them. "The total of Jacob's household who came to Egypt was seventy persons" (Genesis 46:27). However, a funny thing happens when we count the list that enumerates who those individuals were: they total only sixty-nine. Our ancient Rabbis give many answers for whom this list misses, but one interpretation has always struck me as especially profound.

Though she was not born yet, the Bible counts Yocheved, Moses's mother, alongside the other travelers. According to Rabbinic lore, Yocheved was in utero when the Israelites traveled to Egypt, which is why she was numbered but not named (*Genesis Rabbah* 94:9). In fact, they teach that her birth was miraculous; she was born "between the boundary walls," on the precipice of the land of slavery.

As Moses's mother, Yocheved would play the important role of creating, birthing, saving, and nursing the eventual redeemer of Israel. The lesson from Yocheved's birth is simple. Even as we head into our lowest place, our seeds of redemption are already sown. For, even as our ancestors took the ominous steps into Egypt, so optimistic for their future, but so naive in their eventual struggles, the answer to their prayers, not yet uttered, was in place.

As Yocheved was for our ancestors, the seeds of our redemption are already sown. For the many who are suffering among us, the vehicles to carry us out of our loneliness are already before us. They are the inner strength we use to call out from the depths. They are the calm and everlasting presence of family and friends who answer our call. They are those in society who advocate for us and the teachings in our tradition that say that we matter. They are a God who suffers too, yearning for us to reach out our hand toward the Divine. They are the voices of Jeremiah, Hagar, Tamar, and David, the stories of Rachel, Isaac, Moses, and Honi, who can service as companions in our pain. It is the knowledge that communities small and large have struggled as well and have found a way to move forward despite their alienation.

Perhaps more than any of these, our greatest tool to deal with the loneliness in our lives is our hope. Writing in his memoir about struggling with terminal illness, *When Breath Becomes Air*, Paul Kalanithi explains that hope is the marriage of "confidence and desire."[1] When we are lonely, we need the desire to search for a way out of the depth, to call out to loved ones, to seek out relationships, and to journey forward. But simple desire does little without the faith that things will get better, that we can live out the adage of our Talmud "As long as there is life, there is hope" (Jerusalem Talmud, *Berachot* 9:1). Though it may seem dark, there is an end. As our Bible reminds us, "they who sow in tears shall reap with songs of joy" (Psalm 126:5).

For me, Judaism was a wellspring of that hope. As I sought to cope with my loneliness, I found the wisdom of my tradition as a guide. It met me in the darkness and walked with me as I found a way out. It inspired me to call out for help and taught my friends to listen. But I was lucky. I knew where in the tradition to turn. There is a reason that our Rabbis compared their teachings to a "sea." It is frightening in its vastness. Searching our sacred texts without a guide is like navigating the oceans without a map; you may accidently make landfall, but it will be slow and you might end up far from where you intended.

I once had a conversation with a friend who told me about the profound loneliness he faced after the death of his father. Angry and lost, he sought out comfort in Jewish wisdom and community. The more he searched, however, the harder it became. He soon felt that Judaism had nothing to offer his struggle. He found the teachings vapid, the people cold, the congregation unapproachable, and the prayers empty. As time went on, he became alienated from his religion. Judaism, which was supposed to stand for something, suddenly lost its standing. Its voice no longer held power for him.

When we seek out our tradition in life's hardest moments, we need to know that we will find an answer. When my friend called out and did not find a response, he faced two deaths in that moment. Compounded against the death of his father was the death of his faith. Though there is certainly guilt when a loved one passes away, there is no doubt that giving up on the dream of a relevancy to religious truth also brings its own brand of remorse. Crises are the make-or-break moments for religiosity, and when it fails, it fails big.

Our vast tradition does not have all the answers. But it has a voice. It has a presence. It has wisdom, and with the right guide, it can walk beside you toward the light. My hope in writing this book was to identify a few signposts, a story, a text, a teaching, a person to ground us in our struggle with loneliness or with the loneliness of those we love.

When we seek out our faith in its vastness, we don't need to encounter alienation. Its pages and people can escort us on our path to healing.

The beloved Hasidic master Rabbi Chaim of Tsanz once told this parable:

> Once it happened that a man became lost in the depths of a dark forest for many days. At long last, he saw another man approaching him. "Please," he called out to him, "show me the way out of the forest!" "My friend," replied the other, "I too am lost. But I can tell you this: The way I have come from leads nowhere. Let us join hands and search for a new way together."[2]

We have the power to find our way from darkness to light, from desperation to hope, from loneliness to love. We may not know the way out, but we know where we have failed. As we wander, carried by the voices of those who struggled before us, let us do so together.

Notes

Introduction

1. Joseph Heller and Adam J. Sorkin, *Conversations with Joseph Heller* (Jackson, MS: University Press of Mississippi, 1993), 244.

2. *Mishnah Taanit* 3:8. Honi got his name by drawing a circle in the sand and refusing to move until God granted the people rain. Though he was criticized for his brazenness and rashness, the people also admired that God would accede to his request "like a favored child, who sins against his father and is yet forgiven."

3. D. H. Lawrence, *Lady Chatterly's Lover* (New York: Barnes & Noble Classics, 2005), Nook ebook, 178.

Chapter 1: The Nature of Loneliness

1. Steven Greenberg, *Wrestling with God and Man: Homosexuality in the Jewish Tradition* (Madison: University of Wisconsin Press, 2005), 50.

2. There is another classical reason for Eve's creation. Only God can exist alone. By engendering loneliness in Adam, our Rabbis understood that his desire for a wife would send a message to both the angels and future generations of humanity that we are not God and that we have an Achilles' heel: we cannot exist without companionship.

3. John T. Cacioppo and William Patrick, *Loneliness: Human Nature and the Need for Social Connection* (New York: W.W. Norton, 2008); see chap. 1.

4. Peninnah Schram, *Solomon and the Ant: And Other Jewish Folktales* (Honsedale, PA: Boyds Mills Press, 2006), 29.

5. Elizabeth M. Perse and Alan M. Rubin, "Chronic Loneliness and Television Use," *Journal of Broadcasting & Electronic Media* 34, no. 1 (1990): 37–53.

6. Louise C. Hawkley and John T. Cacioppo, "Loneliness Matters: A Theoretical and Empirical Review of Consequences and Mechanisms," *Annals of Behavioral Medicine* 40, no. 2 (2010): 218–27.

7. Emily Caldwell, "Loneliness, Like Chronic Stress, Taxes the Immune System," Research and Innovation Communications, Ohio State University, January 19, 2013, http://researchnews.osu.edu/archive/lonely.htm.

8. Julianne Holt-Lunstad, Timothy Smith, and J. Layton, "Social Relationships and Mortality Risk: A Meta-analytic Review," *SciVee*, doi:10.4016/19865.01.

9. John T. Cacioppo and Louise C. Hawkley, "Perceived Social Isolation and Cognition," *Trends in Cognitive Sciences* 13, no. 10 (2009): 447–54, doi:10.1016/j.tics.2009.06.005.

10. Ian Johnston, "Loneliness Is Becoming a Major Problem in England, Says Church Charity," *Independent*, February 8, 2015, www.independent.co.uk/news/uk/home-news/loneliness-is-becoming-a-major-problem-in-england-says-church-charity-10032639.html.

11. Janice Shaw Crouse, "The Loneliness of American Society," *American Spectator*, May 18, 2014, http://spectator.org/articles/59230/loneliness-american-society.

12. Robert D. Putnam, *Bowling Alone: The Collapse and Revival of American Community* (New York: Simon & Schuster, 2000).

13. Shaw Crouse, "The Loneliness of American Society."

14. Steven M. Cohen and Arnold M. Eisen, "The Sovereign Self: Jewish Identity in Post-Modern America," *Jerusalem Letter/Viewpoints*, Jerusalem Center for Public Affairs, May 1, 2001, www.jcpa.org/jl/vp453.htm.

15. Steven M. Cohen and Arnold M. Eisen, *The Jew Within: Self, Family, and Community in America* (Bloomington: Indiana University Press, 2000).

16. Joel Stein, "Millennials: The Me Me Me Generation," *Time*, May 9, 2013, http://content.time.com/time/subscriber/article/0,33009,2143001,00.html.

17. Margie Warrell, "Text or Talk: Is Technology Making You Lonely?" *Forbes*, May 24, 2012, www.forbes.com/sites/womensmedia/2012/05/24/text-or-talk-is-technology-making-you-lonely/#79c15cab436e.

18. Sherry Turkle, *Alone Together: Why We Expect More from Technology and Less from Each Other* (New York: Basic Books, 2011).

19. Sherry Turkle, "Connected, but Alone?," *TED*, February 2012, https://ted.com/talks/sherry_turkle_alone_together?language=en.

20. Henry David Thoreau, *Walden and Civil Disobedience* (New York: Barnes & Noble Classics, 2003), Nook ebook, 46.

21. Nachman of Breslov, *Magid Sichot* 48.

22. Nachman of Breslov, *The Empty Chair: Finding Hope and Joy: Timeless Wisdom from a Hasidic Master, Rebbe Nachman of Breslov*, adapted by Moshe Mykoff and the Breslov Research Institute (Woodstock, VT: Jewish Lights, 1994), 86.

23. T. D. Wilson et al., "Just Think: The Challenges of the Disengaged Mind," *Science* 345, no. 6192 (2014): 75–77, doi:10.1126/science.1250830.

24. Arthur Green, *Tormented Master: The Life and Spiritual Quest of Rabbi Nachman of Bratslav* (Woodstock VT: Jewish Lights 1992), Nook ebook, 50.

25. Ibid, 50.

26. F. Scott Fitzgerald, *The Great Gatsby* (New York: Scribner, 2004), 55.

27. Joseph B. Soloveitchik, *Lonely Man of Faith* (New York: Random House LLC, 2009).

Chapter 2: The Loneliness of Love

1. *Shulchan Aruch, Even Ha'ezer* 9:1. According to classical Jewish law, if a woman outlives two husbands, she is barred from marrying another lest it was some stain on her that caused their deaths.

2. Melchizedek appeared earlier in Genesis 14, when he fed Abram and blessed him in the name of *El Elyon*, who many commentators see as God. By making Tamar his daughter, the Rabbis were giving her a distinguished place among the nations.

3. Nachmanides, *Emunah U'Bitachon*, chap. 24.

4. While it is understood that this reference is an anachronism and the modern understanding of the chuppah was not yet developed during Tamar's time, there is an assumed authority on the part of commentators, who are given liberties to read their religious norms into the lives of biblical characters.

5. Pamela Druckerman, "What You Learn in Your 40s," *New York Times*, February 28, 2014, www.nytimes.com/2014/03/01/opinion/sunday/what-you-learn-in-your-40s.html?_r=0.

6. Jennifer Senior, *All Joy and No Fun: The Paradox of Modern Parenthood* (New York: Ecco, 2014), 30.

7. These interpretations range from idol worship, to taunting and violence against Isaac, to sexual molestation.

8. Meir Shalev, *Beginnings: Reflections on the Bible's Intriguing Firsts* (New York: Harmony 2011), Nook ebook, 77.

9. Hillel and Shammai debate what this "obnoxious thing" (*ervat davar*) might be. Shammai interprets it narrowly—only sexual impropriety can be grounds for such a divorce. Hillel gives more leeway to the husband—he can divorce his wife for a number of reasons, even ruining dinner. Rabbi Akiva, however, says that he may even divorce her if he finds favor with someone else (Talmud, *Gittin* 90a).

10. The Rabbis debate the meaning of the verse "For a hateful one put away" (Malachi 2:16): "Rabbi Judah said: [This means that] if you hate her you should put her away. Rabbi Johanan says: It means, He that sends his wife away is hated" (Talmud, *Gittin* 90b).

11. The Rabbis understood this irony but took a different tact. They see Ishmael as sick at the time of his expulsion, which is why he was carried by his mother. See *Genesis Rabbah* 53:13.

Chapter 3: The Loneliness of Leadership

1. Abraham Joshua Heschel, *The Prophets: Two Volumes in One* (Peabody, MA: Hendrickson, 2007), 18.

2. See Jeremiah 37:11–16. After a war with the Babylonians, Jeremiah was accused of deserting to the Babylonian side. However, he was probably imprisoned as a reaction to his threat that even if they won in war against them, their enemy would return and destroy the kingdom. He was imprisoned and beaten and freed only after King Zedekiah sent for him.

3. Martin Luther King, "Letter from a Birmingham Jail," April 16, 1963, https://www.africa.upenn.edu/Articles_Gen/Letter_Birmingham.html

4. Ibid.

5. Thomas J. Saporito. "It's Time to Acknowledge CEO Loneliness," Harvard Business Review, February 15, 2012, https://hbr.org/2012/02/its-time-to-acknowledge-ceo-lo

6. Chuck Klosterman, *Eating the Dinosaur* (New York: Scribner, 2010), 71–72.

7. Philip Roth, *Reading Myself and Others* (New York: Farrar, Straus and Giroux, 2013), 100.

Chapter 4: The Loneliness of Sickness and Loss

1. Herman Melville, *Moby Dick* (New York: Barnes & Noble, 2003), Nook ebook, 751.

2. Janet Jaffe, Martha Diamond, and David Diamond, *Unsung Lullabies: Understanding and Coping with Infertility* (New York: St. Martin's Griffin, 2005); see chap. 2.

3. Susan Sontag, *Illness as Metaphor and AIDS and Its Metaphors* (New York: Anchor Books, 1990), 3.

4. Sherwin B. Nuland, *How We Die: Reflections on Life's Final Chapter* (New York: Random House, 1995), xvi.

5. Eighty is the only age that seems to have a positive attribute. This is the age according to our tradition that we receive a "renewed strength."

6. Rashi on Numbers 20:12.

7. Rabbi Isaac Abarbanel on *Parshat Chukkat*.

8. See Deuteronomy 3:23–25, where Moses says, "Sovereign God, you have begun to show to Your servant Your greatness and Your strong hand. For what god is there in heaven or on earth who can do the deeds and mighty

works You do? Let me go over and see the good land beyond the Jordan—that fine hill country and Lebanon" (NIV).

9. Our ancient rabbi Antigonos of Socho was right when he warned us, "Do not be as servants who serve the Master to receive reward. Rather, be as servants who serve the Master not to receive reward."

Chapter 5: Our Lonely God

1. See most notably Maimonides' thirteen principles of faith.

2. James Weldon Johnson, ed., *The Book of American Negro Poetry* (Charleston, SC: BiblioLife, 2008), 94.

3. Based on Ezekiel 1:1–2:8. See *Pirke D'Rabbi Eliezer* 4.

4. God's first command to humanity was "Be fertile and increase" (Genesis 1:28).

5. Based on the verse "From the voices of many waters the mighty breakers of the sea" (Psalm 93:4, translation mine).

6. See D. Kahneman and A. Tversky, "Choices, Values, and Frames," *American Psychologist* 39, no. 4 (1984): 341–50, for the first article published on this topic. In other words, people would rather avoid the risk that would cause them to lose fifty dollars than to embrace that same risk if it might lead to one hundred dollars. This is called risk aversion.

7. See earlier in the chapter, *Genesis Rabbah* 19:7.

8. This is a somewhat creative reading on the original midrash, which sees Moses holding God and proclaiming, "I will not let You be until You pardon and forgive Israel."

9. *Tosafot* on *Shabbat* 116a; see also Ramban on Numbers 10:35.

10. See Rashi on Leviticus 26:15.

11. This quote comes after the Metatron saga, but for the sake of narrative I have put it first.

12. Kalonymus Kalman Shapira, *Esh Kadosh*, (Jerusalem: 1960), 159–64. For fuller description of this idea on Esh Kadosh see Nehemia Polen, *The Holy Fire: The Teachings of Rabbi Kalonymus Kalman Shapira, the Rebbe of the Warsaw Ghetto* (Lanham, MD: Jason Aronson Inc. 1999), 106–121.

13. Abraham Joshua Heschel, *Man Is Not Alone* (New York: Farrar, Straus and Giroux, 1976), 154.

14. Abraham Joshua Heschel, *God in Search of Man* (New York: Farrar, Straus and Giroux, 1976), 137.

Chapter 6: Israel, the Lonely People

1. See Talmud, *Chulin* 5a, which says that profaning Shabbat in public is one of the few acts that define a Jew as an apostate, and since we have the statement

Af al pi shechat yisrael hu, "Even if he sins, he is still a Jew" (Talmud, *Sanhedrin* 44a), the act of leaving Judaism is akin to other sins like idolatry.

2. Rambam on Genesis 12:10. Technically, Nachmanides believed the big sin Abraham committed was his leaving Canaan in the first place, but Abraham's lie facilitated this abandonment of the land and was therefore an important ingredient in God's anger.

3. Simon Rawidowicz, "Israel: The Ever-Dying People," in *State of Israel, Diaspora, and Jewish Continuity: Essays on the "Ever-Dying People"* (Waltham, MA: Brandeis University Press, 1998), 63.

4. Micah Goodman, *Maimonides and the Book That Changed Judaism: Secrets of the Guide for the Perplexed* (Philadelphia: Jewish Publication Society, 2015), 33.

Chapter 7: From the Depths

1. Maimonides, *Mishneh Torah, Hilchot Shofar* 3:2

2. Nassim Nicholas Taleb, *Antifragile: Things That Gain from Disorder* (New York: Random House, 2012).

3. Nachman of Breslov, *Likutei Moharan* 4:5.

4. See Brene Brown, "Listening to Shame," TED, March 2012, http://www.ted.com /talks/brene_brown_listening_to_shame.

5. See Isaiah 49:8; Ezekiel 33:28.

6. *Zohar*, Exodus 20a. Translation found in Lawrence A. Hoffman, ed., *My People's Prayer Book*, vol. 2, *The Amidah* (Woodstock, VT: Jewish Lights, 1997), 2.

7. Elimelech of Lizhensk, *Noam Elimelech, Parshat Va'eira*.

8. This folk saying is potentially apocryphal but usually attributed to Rav Abraham Isaac Kook (source unknown).

Chapter 8: Hearing the Call

1. Rashi to 1 Samuel 28:8.

2. Part of her strength was in convincing his men to keep urging him to eat. Later in the chapter (and book) we will discuss the importance of helping others to notice and aid the suffering around them.

3. Robert Alter, *David Story: A Translation with Commentary of 1 and 2 Samuel* (New York: W. W. Norton, 2009), 178.

4. David Wolpe, *David: The Divided Heart* (New Haven, CT: Yale University Press, 2014), 45.

5. For the best study about the pathos of the book of Job, see Harold Kushner, *The Book of Job: When Bad Things Happened to a Good Person*, Jewish Encounters Series (New York: Schocken Books, 2012).

6. I am thankful to Rabbi Rachel Timoner for teaching me this text.

7. Leo Tolstoy, *The Death of Ivan Ilych*, trans. Ian Dreiblatt (Brooklyn, NY: Melville House, 2008), 70.

8. Atul Gawande, *Being Mortal: Medicine and What Matters in the End* (New York: Metropolitan Books, 2014), 90.

9. Brené Brown, "Brené Brown on Empathy," RSA Shorts, December 10, 2013, YouTube video, www.youtube.com/watch?v=1Evwgu369Jw.

10. Nissim ben Jacob Ibn Shahin, *An Elegant Composition Concerning Relief after Death*, trans. William M. Brenner (New Haven, CT: Yale University Press, 1997), 5; original story expanded from Talmud, *Taanit* 22a.

11. Baal Shem Tov, *Keter Shem Tov*, 272.

12. In truth, this may not be exactly what the Baal Shem Tov meant. His words could also be taken to mean that when we suffer, we can't understand our place in God's plan. Classical Jewish theology sees a purpose to everything that happens in life. Nevertheless, the image of levity lifting us outside of our suffering for perspective is the salient point of his statement, and therefore we do not need to include the more complicating theological valiance that might only serve to alienate those who suffer.

13. Daniel Gilbert, *Stumbling on Happiness* (New York: Knopf Doubleday, 2006), 21.

14. See also *Sifrei* on Numbers, chap. 99.

Chapter 9: The Communal Response to Loneliness

1. A *mamzer* is the product of a union that should not be.

2. Ta-Nehisi Coates, *Between the World and Me* (New York: Spiegal & Grau, 2015), 113.

3. Wyatt Mason, "Make This Not True," *New York Review of Books*, February 6, 2014, www.nybooks.com/articles/2014/02/06/george-saunders-make-this-not-true/.

4. Ibn Shahin, *An Elegant Composition Concerning Relief after Death*, 76.

5. Ibid.

6. For the full text, see Elyse D. Frishman, ed., *Mishkan T'filah: A Reform Siddur* (New York: CCAR Press, 2007), 579.

Chapter 10: Sacred Searching

1. Pinchas Sadeh, *Jewish Folktales*, trans. Hillel Halkin (New York: Anchor Books, 1989), 381.

2. Jonathan Sacks, ed., *The Koren Siddur* (Jerusalem: Koren, 2009), xliii.

3. I first encountered this quote in Harold Kushner's forward to Viktor Frankl, *Man's Search for Meaning* (Boston: Beacon Press, 2006).

4. Emily Dickinson, "If I Can Stop One Heart from Breaking," *The Complete Poems of Emily Dickinson* (New York: Barnes & Noble Classics, 2003), 42.

Conclusion

1. Paul Kalanithi, *When Breath Becomes Air* (New York: Random House LLC, 2016), 133.

2. I am indebted to my childhood rabbi, James Rosenberg, who often told this story at *Kabbalat Shabbat* services.

Suggestions for Further Learning

Brown, Brené. "Brené Brown on Empathy," RSA Shorts, December 10, 2013, You-Tube video, www.youtube.com/watch?v=1Evwgu369Jw.

Cacioppo, John T. and William Patrick, *Loneliness: Human Nature and the Need for Social Connection*. New York: W.W. Norton, 2008.

Cohen, Steven M. and Arnold M. Eisen. *The Jew Within: Self, Family, and Community in America*. Bloomington: Indiana University Press, 2000.

Coates, Ta-Nehisi. *Between the World and Me*. New York: Spiegal & Grau, 2015.

Frankel, Estelle. *Sacred Therapy: Jewish Spiritual Teachings on Emotional Healing and Inner Wholeness*. Boston: Shambhala, 2005.

Frankl, Viktor. *Man's Search for Meaning*. Boston: Beacon Press, 2006.

Gawande, Atul. *Being Mortal: Medicine and What Matters in the End*. New York: Metropolitan Books, 2014.

Gilbert, Daniel. *Stumbling on Happiness*. New York: Knopf Doubleday, 2006.

Green, Arthur. *Tormented Master: The Life and Spiritual Quest of Rabbi Nachman of Bratslav*. Woodstock VT: Jewish Lights, 1992.

Greenberg, Steven. *Wrestling with God and Man: Homosexuality in the Jewish Tradition*. Madison: University of Wisconsin Press, 2005.

Heschel, Abraham Joshua. *God in Search of Man: A Philosophy of Judaism*. New York: Farrar, Straus and Giroux, 1976.

———. *Man Is Not Alone*. New York: Farrar, Straus and Giroux, 1976.

———. *The Prophets: Two Volumes in One*. Peabody, MA: Hendrickson, 2007.

Jaffe, Janet, Martha Diamond, and David Diamond, *Unsung Lullabies: Understanding and Coping with Infertility*. New York: St. Martin's Griffin, 2005

Kushner, Harold. *The Book of Job: When Bad Things Happened to a Good Person*, Jewish Encounters Series. New York: Schocken Books, 2012.

———. *When Bad Things Happen to Good People*. New York: Anchor Books, 2007.

Meszler, Joseph. *Facing Illness, Finding God: How Judaism Can Help You and Caregivers Cope When Body or Spirit Fails*. Woodstock, VT: Jewish Lights, 2010.

Michaelson, Jay. *The Gate of Tears: Sadness and the Spiritual Path*. Teaneck, NJ: Ben Yehuda Press, 2015.

Nachman of Breslov. *The Empty Chair: Finding Hope and Joy: Timeless Wisdom from a Hasidic Master, Rebbe Nachman of Breslov*, adapted by Moshe Mykoff and the Breslov Research Institute. Woodstock, VT: Jewish Lights, 1994.

Nouwen, Henri J. M. *The Wounded Healer: Ministry in Contemporary Society*. New York: Image Books, 1979.

Putnam, Robert D. *Bowling Alone: The Collapse and Revival of American Community*. New York: Simon & Schuster, 2000.

Shalev, Meir. *Beginnings: Reflections on the Bible's Intriguing Firsts*. New York: Harmony, 2011.

Soloveitchik, Joseph B. *Lonely Man of Faith*. New York: Random House, 2006.

Sontag, Susan. *Illness as Metaphor and AIDS and Its Metaphors*. New York: Anchor Books, 1990.

Turkle, Sherry. *Alone Together: Why We Expect More from Technology and Less from Each Other*. New York: Basic Books, 2011.

Weintraub, Simkha. *Healing of Soul, Healing of Body: Spiritual Leaders Unfold the Strength & Solace in Psalms*. Woodstock, VT: Jewish Lights, 2009.

Wolpe, David. *David: The Divided Heart*. New Haven, CT: Yale University Press, 2014.

About the Author

RABBI MARC KATZ is the Associate Rabbi at Congregation Beth Elohim in Park Slope, Brooklyn. He was ordained at Hebrew Union College - Jewish Institute of Religion. Rabbi Katz has written for numerous publications including *Tablet Magazine*, the *CCAR Journal*, and is a contributing writer for *The Sacred Encounter: Jewish Perspectives on Sexuality*. He lives in Park Slope with his wife Ayelet Nelson.

CPSIA information can be obtained
at www.ICGtesting.com
Printed in the USA
JSHW061547120523
41644JS00001B/26